D0436777

first names

BEYONCÉ

Nansubuga Nagadya Isdahl

Illustrations by Tammy Taylor

Abrams Books for Young Readers

NEW YORK

First Names: *Beyoncé* is not an official biography,
but it has been carefully checked and the facts are
accurate to the best of our knowledge. However,
if you spot something you think may be incorrect,
please let us know. Some of the passages in this book
are actual quotes from Beyoncé and other people.
You'll be able to tell which ones they are by the style
of type: *I was served lemons, but I made lemonade.*

Library of Congress Control Number 2020947153

ISBN 978-1-4197-5371-8

Text copyright © 2021 Nansubuga Nagadya Isdahl
Illustrations copyright © 2021 Tammy Taylor
Book design by Charice Silverman

2020 © as UK edition. First published in 2020
by David Fickling Books Limited

Published under license from David Fickling Books Limited.
Published in 2021 by Abrams Books for Young Readers, an imprint of
ABRAMS. All rights reserved. No portion of this book may be reproduced,
stored in a retrieval system, or transmitted in any form or by any means,
mechanical, electronic, photocopying, recording, or otherwise, without
written permission from the publisher.

Printed and bound in U.S.A.
10 9 8 7 6 5 4 3 2 1

Abrams Books for Young Readers are available at special discounts when
purchased in quantity for premiums and promotions as well as fundraising
or educational use. Special editions can also be created to specification. For
details, contact specialsales@abramsbooks.com or the address below.

Abrams® is a registered trademark of Harry N. Abrams, Inc.

ABRAMS The Art of Books
195 Broadway, New York, NY 10007
abramsbooks.com

CONTENTS

INTRODUCTION—Beyoncé Sings a Song

THE PLACE: St. Mary's Talent Show, Houston, Texas
THE TIME: 1988

The school auditorium was so hot Beyoncé felt she could have burst into flames. Poking her head through the curtains, she saw a sea of people waving their programs around like fans. There was nothing that seven-year-old Beyoncé could think of that would help her cool down, though.

With her heart pounding as loud as a drum, her nerves were almost getting the better of her. She wished she could disappear. But it was too late now. **It was her turn to sing!**

"Take a deep breath," her teacher, Miss Darlette, told her as she gave her hand a squeeze. Then she pushed Beyoncé forward.

The microphone was only a few feet away from her, but it might as well have been on the moon. Beyoncé's feet felt like they were dragging through sludge, but finally, she made it. Now all she had to do was summon up the courage to sing.

Beyoncé was used to family sing-alongs at home with her mom, dad, and sister. Those were always a blast. But this was her very first talent show . . . her very first time onstage in front of a large audience. It was new—scary—territory.

As Beyoncé stood frozen in front of the wilting audience, the music started. **And then a miracle happened.** *Poof*, like magic, her pesky nerves were gone . . . and something else, something much bigger, replaced them. Little Beyoncé dug deep inside herself and, spreading her arms wide, she found the courage to sing. Her incredible voice carried John Lennon's "Imagine" around the hall, and the audience were suddenly wide awake, sitting bolt upright in their seats. Beyoncé's nerves were completely forgotten.

As the song drew to a close, the audience erupted. Everyone was on their feet! Disaster averted, and Beyoncé was in seventh heaven. She'd gotten a standing ovation and totally stolen the show.

Her parents, meanwhile, were in total shock. They hadn't even seen their little girl rehearse!

That can't be our Beyoncé.

But it was. Beyoncé had just found her voice.

She won the talent show, of course. Then she went on to win another, and another, and another. In fact, by the time Beyoncé was thirty-five years old, **she'd won about a gazillion awards** (OK, more like three hundred) . . . she'd had several record-breaking world tours . . . a leading role in an Academy Award–winning movie . . . and she owned her own entertainment company! The list of achievements goes on, and today it seems like Beyoncé has it all: money, fame, success . . .

Hang on, that's not why I did it. I just wanted to give my all and share my gifts with the world.

And now you perform in front of hundreds of thousands of people. How on earth did you get over your stage fright?

Oh, I never really did! It's just that I don't let it stop me. Nerves show that I care.

That's true, and you're certainly well-known for working harder than anyone else in your industry.

Well, I had to give up a lot of my childhood, but I feel like I was born to be a performer. And that's the thing about achieving your dreams—you have to sacrifice a lot, work hard, never make excuses, and never, ever give up . . .

Sounds exhausting! And still, you never seem to miss a beat.

Oh, I've missed a few beats . . .

Really—when?

Y'all better read on, and find out!

1   BEYONCÉ PUTS ON A SHOW

Beyoncé Knowles made her grand entrance into the world on September 4, 1981, in Houston, Texas. According to her mom, giving birth was the easy part—naming her baby turned out to be more complicated. Quite a few family eyebrows were raised when her mom announced . . .

Beyoncé's mom, Celestine Beyincé Knowles (better known as Tina), wanting to keep her roots alive, had made an adjustment to her own family's name for her firstborn child. The rest of the family had their doubts, and once she was old enough to have an opinion, **Beyoncé herself wasn't exactly thrilled.**

Whatever name she preferred, Bey or Beyoncé basked in the love of her doting parents. It was nearly five years before the family expanded, giving Beyoncé a baby sister, Solange. Beyoncé was a dutiful and protective big sister, helping with the baby right from the start. The two girls always stuck together.

The Knowles family was pretty well off. Their dad, Mathew, earned a good living as a sales executive for the Xerox Corporation (inventors of the first photocopier) while their mom, Tina, owned a happening hair salon called Headliners. A few years after she was born, Beyoncé's parents moved into a roomy six-bedroom house in Houston's well-to-do Third Ward neighborhood. They drove nice cars, the girls went to private schools, and the family even had a housekeeper!

But Beyoncé's parents hadn't always lived so comfortably. Tina and Mathew came from poor families in the South, which had a terrible history of racist laws. They were born at a time when racial prejudice and discrimination were a part of everyday life, when African Americans were still fighting for their civil rights. So they both understood how important it was to work hard and **make something of whatever you had**—which was a message they'd pass on to their daughters.

When Tina's parents couldn't afford to pay the tuition fees for her Catholic school, her mom, Agnèz, had paid her way by sewing clothes for the priests and the nuns who worked there and making uniforms for the other students. She made sure Tina knew how to sew, and those skills came in handy as Beyoncé and Solange were growing up!

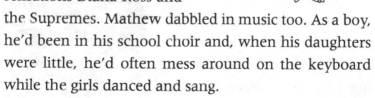

♩ Wooo ♫

♪ Wooo

Woooo ♂

♫

What Tina and Mathew also had in common was a love of music.

In her teens, Beyoncé's mom had sung in a pop group called the Veltones, inspired by 1960s all-female singing sensations Diana Ross and the Supremes. Mathew dabbled in music too. As a boy, he'd been in his school choir and, when his daughters were little, he'd often mess around on the keyboard while the girls danced and sang.

Music was as much a part of homelife for the Knowles family as the air they breathed. Sunday dinners were often followed by another family tradition: grooving and singing along to Mom and Dad's record collection. Prince and Michael Jackson were firm family favorites.

Beyoncé danced before she could walk (around age one).

She sang with her father as he played the keyboard (around age five).

She really loved singing gospel music in the church choir (around age seven).

One day, not long after she started school, Tina asked Beyoncé what she'd learned. *"A song,"* said Beyoncé.

"Well, that's nice. Let's hear it," said Tina. As little Bey proudly sang to her mom, she experienced **a rush of excitement** she'd never felt before!

Hmm, not bad!

This is fun!

She may have had a big voice at home, but away from her family and close friends, Beyoncé was quiet and shy. She had an especially hard time at school.

A few of her classmates made fun of her because her skin was lighter than some of the other girls' and mocked her for having big ears!

They ARE big, I look like Dumbo the elephant.

Perfectly normal-sized ears.

Beyoncé just didn't fit in, and it turned out Grandad was right; her unique name didn't help. She struggled with her schoolwork too, and with all the bullying and teasing, she often **wished she could just hide under a rock**.

Sending Beyoncé to dance classes at Darlette Johnson's dance studio was Tina and Mathew's solution. They thought it might help build up her confidence.

Beyoncé loved it. Sometimes she danced so hard that she ripped her costumes apart at the seams.

Often the last one to leave, Beyoncé was hanging around after class one day, when she heard Miss Darlette singing a song slightly out of tune. Without a second thought, Beyoncé joined in, finishing the song. She must have sounded pretty good, because Miss Darlette asked her to sing it again.

When Tina and Mathew came to pick her up that day, Miss Darlette was full of excitement. *"She can sing! You know, she really* can *sing,"* she said. Miss Darlette was convinced that **Beyoncé had something special**, and soon she was encouraging her to perform a John Lennon song in that very first talent show that she went on to win.

In spite of her nerves, from her first show onward, Beyoncé was hooked on performing—and she was 100 percent sure it was what she wanted to do.

Practice Makes Perfect

Not many kids have their future mapped out from the age of seven, and Beyoncé's parents weren't quite sure what to make of it. But they could see how much their daughter loved the stage, so they enrolled her in more competitions. And the more she entered, the more she wanted to enter!

A lot of the competitions were just glorified beauty pageants with a talent section, and being a tomboy at heart, **Beyoncé hated having to be primped and preened** with ruffles, flounces, and frills.

> If I have to wear one more bow, I'll . . .

But although it was the talent portion she loved, she couldn't win without entering the beauty part.

After one year of competitions, Beyoncé's bedroom was overflowing with trophies. Some were as tall as she was . . . one or two were even taller! She had so many that she could barely walk around her room without knocking one over.

Her sister's success must have puzzled little Solange because, one day, she took care of the annoying trophy problem by cheerfully taking apart every single one she could get her tiny hands on. When Beyoncé found her, Solange was sitting among the wreckage of at least thirty of them.

Ha, ha, very funny, Solange, but now you've got to put them all back together.

With the trophies piling up, though, Beyoncé's parents realized that nothing was going to stop their firstborn from following her dream. They quickly jumped on board and decided **they would do whatever they could to help her**.

Mathew spent time with her practicing and perfecting her routines before her shows, while Tina searched for professional singing lessons. If Beyoncé was serious about this, she might as well get proper voice training.

Tina found a local coach named David Lee Brewer. When he first met the sweet little eight-year-old (wearing a frilly dress and matching socks), David was amazed. Beyoncé opened her mouth and nearly knocked him over with the power of her voice. There was no question about taking her on. At one point, David even moved in, living over the Knowles's garage so **Beyoncé could have lessons on demand**. Even outside voice lessons, Beyoncé could belt out tunes all day long with the help of a karaoke machine.

BEDROOMS AND BACKYARDS

Beyoncé had all the comforts of a happy childhood: fun family Christmases; summer-long sleepovers with her favorite cousin, Angie; a pair of pink cowboy boots that her mom had to peel off her she loved them so much; and trips to the local Livestock Show and Rodeo (along with the obligatory deep-fried Snickers bar)!

Mmm, this is what we REALLY came for . . .

Cowboy boots, last taken off seven days ago

Mostly, though, Beyoncé and Solange were happiest putting on a show. They would practice together almost every day. Beyoncé worked on her routines in her bedroom mirror **over and over again** until she was totally breathless. She wanted to get them as polished as Janet Jackson's.

JANET JACKSON

Born 1966
Singer/songwriter,
dancer, actor, choreographer

Janet Jackson's big bro was none other than Michael Jackson, the King of Pop, but she also had a massive following. Her singing career skyrocketed in the 1980s and 1990s. With the help of big pop hits like "Control" and "Rhythm Nation," she sold over 180 million records. Beyoncé wasn't just amazed by her singing; her dancing was incredible too. Her performances were larger than life, her choreography spectacular!

Taking matters into their own hands, the sisters made a stage out of just about anything: sofa cushions, beds, coffee tables. Nothing was off-limits. Then they'd perform together for anyone who would listen! Maybe it's because their personalities were so different—Solange was sassy and Beyoncé was sweet—but there was never any real rivalry between them. They just did what they loved doing as often as they possibly could!

Most parents would have something to say about their kids jumping on the furniture. But knowing just how much both girls loved to perform, they did something amazing. They built an **out-of-this-world-sized deck** behind the house for Beyoncé and Solange to practice on.

Beyoncé and Solange were thrilled. They used their deck to put on shows as often as they could.

Finally, get all your friends and family to come to the show. Aunts, uncles, cousins . . . Everyone is welcome . . .
But everyone has to pay!

VIPs seven dollars!!

Show tonight $5
VIPS $7

VIP DAD

VIP MOM

We didn't put in all this hard work for nothing, Mom!

Beyoncé lived and breathed performing. She knew how to charm a crowd, blowing kisses to the audience and messing around onstage. **She was a natural.** She loved the sense of freedom she had onstage, and the singing was just so exhilarating.

But at the age of eight, the local audiences were starting to seem too small to Beyoncé. While other kids were still dressing up, she was thinking about how to make her dreams come true . . . in the real world.

I wanted to be a star!

2   BEYONCÉ GETS A BREAK

When eight-year-old Beyoncé got the opportunity to perform at the People's Workshop—a big annual talent competition that gave kids a chance to show off to local music and entertainment bigwigs—she took it. She didn't know where it might lead, but she gave it her all, as always. Who knew when a big break might be just around the corner?

As it turns out, two ladies saw Beyoncé performing that day and were very impressed. They were actually getting ready to put a girl group together and they were looking to audition some fresh talent. They didn't just want girls who could sing and dance, though. **They wanted charisma**, and Beyoncé had it! Everyone agreed, she just had to try out.

THE GIRLS GET TOGETHER

About fifty to sixty hopefuls showed up for the audition, including a girl named LaTavia Roberson, a young rapper and dancer who could sing too. Beyoncé and LaTavia were two of the lucky ones. They made the cut, and a band called Girls Tyme was born. Beyoncé's dreams of becoming a REAL performer might actually be coming true.

It took some time to get everything together, and Girls Tyme had a few rough patches at the start, especially when it came to keeping members in the group. At one point, they had twelve members, then they shrank back down to five, and eventually the band consisted of Beyoncé, LaTavia, sisters Nikki and Nina Taylor (LaTavia's cousins), and Ashley Támar Davis.

Soon after, another girl joined the group: Kelly Rowland. **Kelly and Beyoncé had a lot in common**: they were the same age, they both loved to sing (Kelly had been in the church choir since she was four years old), and they both dreamed of becoming famous singers. And they loved pop diva Whitney Houston.

Whitney was our idol.

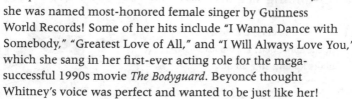

WHITNEY HOUSTON

1963–2012
Singer and actor

Whitney Houston was one of the world's most famous singers. She racked up so many awards—more than 400—that she was named most-honored female singer by Guinness World Records! Some of her hits include "I Wanna Dance with Somebody," "Greatest Love of All," and "I Will Always Love You," which she sang in her first-ever acting role for the mega-successful 1990s movie *The Bodyguard*. Beyoncé thought Whitney's voice was perfect and wanted to be just like her!

Kelly had recently moved to Houston with her mom. She'd had a pretty tough childhood. Her father was no longer in the picture and her mom was struggling to make ends meet as a live-in nanny. Kelly had also been bullied at her old school (another thing the girls had in common). But Kelly was determined to succeed.

Performing had given Beyoncé confidence onstage, but **offstage she was still shy and quiet**. She'd never had very many friends. Being in a girl band with a group of kids who all shared the same hopes and dreams changed all that.

KELLY AND BEY

The girls spent a lot of time together and Kelly quickly became like a second sister to Beyoncé. They'd practice dancing and harmonizing together while Kelly's mom worked around the clock. They even went to the same school. In the end, it made sense for Kelly to move in with the Knowles family, though her mom came over every night to kiss her good night. For Kelly and Beyoncé, life became one huge, never-ending sleepover!

☆ We were so close we slept in the same bed! We would wake up and sing all day.

You were singing in your sleep!

☆ We loved to hang out at the pool or watch *The Mickey Mouse Club*—our room was practically a Mickey Mouse museum.

☆ We were also a little naughty . . . We took the mattresses off the beds and used them to slide down the stairs; we made huge swings out of the curtains; when people were asleep, we would put toothpaste and mustard on their faces.

☆ Once we even trapped some cats in the house! Mom came home and found about twenty of them all over the place! Oops . . .

A Super Super Bowl Sunday

In early 1991, when Beyoncé was nine years old, the United States was fighting the Gulf War in the Persian Gulf. The war had taken its toll on the country, and with thousands of troops abroad, many Americans back home wanted something to celebrate. What the country needed was a hearty dose of inspiration, and it came in the form of a football game: Super Bowl XXV in Tampa, Florida.

Millions of people were watching on that warm January night, including the entire Knowles family. But they hadn't tuned in only for the game: Whitney Houston was booked to sing the national anthem. Even though she was an international star at the height of her career, it was still a **huge honor** to be asked.

Beyoncé was glued to the TV screen as Whitney stepped onto the platform, and when she started to sing, **magic happened**. It was like she lifted the crowd with her voice. Whitney put her own unforgettable stamp on "The Star-Spangled Banner." The recording of her performance even made it into the top 20 (since when has a national anthem had a place in the pop charts?).

When Whitney was done, a million cameras seemed to flash at once in the stadium and many people were crying.

At home in front of the TV, Beyoncé was inspired. She turned to her mom and said:

She didn't just want to sing: **she wanted to move people** the way Whitney's singing had just moved her. And she liked the idea of appearing on TV too.

WORKING UNDERCOVER

By this time, Beyoncé had been quietly working away with Girls Tyme for about a year. Bey was like a spy on a top-secret mission. No one outside her close family and friends had any idea that Beyoncé was in a singing group. Even her classmates at Parker Music Academy didn't know, and the school was filled with musical kids just like her!

Beyoncé and Kelly hardly ever hung out with the others, because Girls Tyme practiced for up to eight hours a day—including school days. So they missed out on lots of stuff normal kids were doing. Still shy as

ever at school, once class ended,
Beyoncé ran off to rehearse
with Girls Tyme,
where she could
**show who she
really was**.

When they weren't rehearsing, Beyoncé, Kelly, and Solange would go to WaterWorld or AstroWorld—two nearby theme parks—for a spin on all their favorite rides.

California Dreamin'

Beyoncé had quickly been picked out as lead singer, and when Girls Tyme got a new manager, Andretta Tillman, they started to land some small-time gigs at local venues. Soon they were getting noticed around town. Then one evening in the summer of 1991, Beyoncé came home from rehearsal with some **big news**.

We're heading to California!

Andretta had got in touch with her friend Teresa LaBarbera White, who worked in California for Sony Records, and managed to book the girls a spot at the Gavin Convention—where famous and hoping-to-be-famous people in the music industry got together every year to talk business. It's where deals are made.

Beyoncé and the girls had **five weeks to prepare**. As usual, they rehearsed day and night, made sure they had great outfits . . .

I wanna be Michael.

No, I'm Michael!

We looked a little like The Jacksons (the super cool 70s R&B band that starred the young Michael Jackson) with our sparkly white tuxedo jackets, silk blouses, and bow ties.

. . . and stopped by Headliners for some primping. Now they were all set to take off!

It was the first time any of the girls had been on a plane!

Once they landed, though, they quickly forgot about the flight, because, almost before they knew it, Girls Tyme had to be onstage in those sparkly tuxedos.

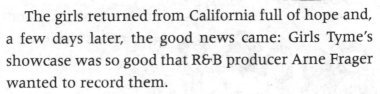

I was terrified that I'd forget the lyrics . . . but I did my best.

The girls returned from California full of hope and, a few days later, the good news came: Girls Tyme's showcase was so good that R&B producer Arne Frager wanted to record them.

In fact, Arne was so impressed, he flew Girls Tyme all the way back to his California recording studios to start plotting their way to stardom. **The girls were so excited**—but they still weren't afraid to tell him what they were after:

A BIG RECORD DEAL!

Hmm. If they wanted to sign with a well-known record label, Arne told them, they needed a big national spotlight.

SEARCHING FOR THE STARS

Today there are countless music competition TV shows. But back when Beyoncé was a kid, there was just one. It was called *Star Search*, and it was **the biggest talent contest** on American TV. If you got lucky, it could launch your career into turbo drive! The show worked like this:

☆ In each of several categories, two acts competed against one another. The champion (the act that had won the previous show) and a newcomer.

☆ A panel of four judges awarded up to four stars to each act. If your act won the highest score, you made it to the next round and the next show. The aim was to keep going to the final round.

☆ At the championship show, the winners were awarded a $100,000 prize. But, more importantly, they got lots of attention—and maybe even a record deal!

Some pretty famous people performed on *Star Search* before they shot off into the stratosphere—Alanis Morissette, Usher, Britney Spears, Justin Timberlake, and Christina Aguilera, to name but a few.

And since Beyoncé had already listed her **three biggest goals** in life:

* Make a gold album
* Record a follow-up platinum album
* Write and produce a third album

. . . finding her way onto a big national talent show seemed worth a shot!

Arne used his connections to get Girls Tyme on *Star Search* and the girls were over the moon. They were also laser-focused. As if they weren't already practicing hard enough, they rehearsed around the clock for months on end before the show.

Their chance finally came toward the end of 1992. The girls traveled to Orlando, Florida (about 1,000 miles away), where the show was recorded. This was their big shot. As far as Beyoncé was concerned, **losing wasn't an option**. She daydreamed about winning the *Star Search* final, then getting the best record deal ever and Girls Tyme going on to become the next supergroup . . .

We're in it to win it!

It was a tough contest, though. They were up against a rock band called Skeleton Crew—the members of that band were at least twice the girls' age and, of course, they were the champions from the previous round. Backstage, while Skeleton Crew performed, the girls were a bundle of nerves. They stood in the dark and said a quick prayer. And then, as soon as they got their cue, they were off. The compère, Ed McMahon, introduced them: "Welcome, Beyoncé, LaTivia [he'd mispronounced LaTavia's name!], Nina, Nicki, Kelly, and Ashley, the hip-hop rapping Girls Tyme."

LaTavia bounced to the front, opening the performance with a rap, while the rest of the girls sashayed across the pink-and-purple-lit stage in colorful rain jackets and matching shorts. LaTavia passed the microphone to Beyoncé, who was hard to miss in her fluorescent green jacket. They'd all poured their hearts into these two-and-a-half minutes and practiced so much. How could they possibly lose?

They had barely caught their breath before it was time to be judged. Girls Tyme stood in a neat row onstage, their **anxiety shooting through the roof**. Beyoncé's heart was hammering in her chest as Mr. McMahon finally announced:

The girls were crushed. They hadn't even made it through the first round! It had taken months of rehearsals—every day of the week—to prepare for the show, but just one minute for Beyoncé's biggest dream to fall apart. The girls smiled politely for the cameras, but as soon as the show cut for the commercial break, they all ran offstage and **cried their eyes out**. Their confidence was shattered along with their hopes of ever getting a record deal.

> That's when I realized, however good you are, sometimes you just lose.

Never Give Up

A few months later when the show aired, Tina cooked up a huge pot of her famous gumbo. She'd invited the entire family over for a surprise party to watch Beyoncé's very first TV appearance. The trouble was, it had been an embarrassing letdown. Imagine how

Beyoncé must have felt to relive that defeat again in front of all her loved ones.

Bey's parents were still incredibly proud of how much she had achieved. If she really wanted to perform, they told her, she shouldn't let one TV show stop her!

However, after watching the video of their performance, Beyoncé had to admit, **it hadn't exactly been amazing**. For starters, the song was wrong. Hip-hop didn't show off their fantastic singing voices, one of the girls had forgotten a dance step, another one had sung off key. . .

Beyoncé didn't stay down for too long. She didn't need sympathy, she realized, she needed to work even harder. If the girls had any chance of making it, they needed to polish up their routines big time.

The trick is to always, ALWAYS, pick yourself up again and learn from what went wrong.

Watching the girls perform on that stage, **a plan was hatching in Mathew's mind**. He knew they had something special, and he was ready to give the group all he had!

He pleaded with Andretta to let him step in and manage Girls Tyme alongside her—some say he even threatened to pull Beyoncé if Andretta didn't agree! However it happened, now that Mathew was at least half in charge, he had some ideas about what the girls needed to do next.

KNOWLES BOOTCAMP

Getting straight down to business, Mathew and Andretta agreed the lineup needed to change. There were too many girls in the band and they didn't quite gel. So they reduced the group to just four members:

Kelly Rowland: As well as being Beyoncé's best friend and her second sister, she's the sensitive one—always first to cry over weepy movies. LaTavia noticed her singing talent first, when they were playing Barbies!

Beyoncé Knowles: Big voice and a bundle of nerves! The mamma of the group—always looking out for everyone.

LaTavia Roberson: The sassiest of the four A rapping and dancing sensation, she'd been a child model before she joined Girls Tyme.

LeToya Luckett: The newbie and the group's joker. Beyoncé's classmate and fellow star of their school play, *Pinocchio*.

The group's name needed some attention too. After LeToya joined, the girls tried Somethin' Fresh . . . then Borderline . . . then Cliché . . . They settled on The Dolls for a while. But nothing had the commercial appeal, or the *pizzazz* they were looking for.

The name could wait, though. It was time to get

to work! Mathew meant business. And by business
he meant bootcamp:

⭐ The girls had to be up at 6 a.m. to go for a run (while singing!).

⭐ Pizza and French fries were out; healthy meals were in.

⭐ They had to practice their complicated dance moves in high heels
(ouch!).

⭐ They had to perform
in front of a real live
audience once a week.

For nearly two years, Mathew pushed the girls
through this **back-breaking routine**. But for the most
part, Beyoncé didn't mind. The hard work may have
cost her a normal childhood, but it was helping her
achieve her dream.

Beyoncé and the group hung out at Tina's salon whenever they had a spare moment, mostly practicing their routines—they couldn't stop! It didn't always go down well with the clients.

Tina made sure the girls picked up some brooms and helped sweep up too.

The salon also came in handy for Beyoncé's songwriting. She'd been working on lyrics of her own for a while—Mathew thought it was good practice for the girls to compose their own songs, and Beyoncé seemed to have a knack for it. It was also a great way for her to let out her feelings. She made good use of the stories she overheard at Headliners—they were **the juiciest she knew**. She'd plop herself down quietly in the corner and eavesdrop on tales of love and heartbreak, backstabbing and wrongdoing. It was like a real-life romance novel.

FINALLY, A BIG BREAK?

By the time Beyoncé was twelve, in 1993, she and the girls felt they were ready to record an album. But the group still hadn't struck a deal. Mathew had sent out heaps of demos, but he was struggling to get anyone who could actually make a difference to listen.

Finally, he landed the girls a slot at the Black Expo in Houston, a local trade fair and festival, where there'd be executives from top record labels on the lookout for talent. **The girls hit the jackpot.** The successful Atlanta-based producer Daryl Simmons heard them sing and jumped on board, using his connections to recommend the group to an actual record label: Elektra Records.

After a lot of waiting and some more auditions, **the girls had a deal**. They couldn't believe it! Elektra Records was a major music label. It seemed like they were on their way at last.

Whoop! Yay, we did it!

They want you!

The group signed a contract in 1995 and soon afterward they flew 800 miles (1,200 km) to Atlanta, Georgia, to record their very first album.

Their schedule was grinding. If they thought Mathew's bootcamp was hard, now they understood what real pressure was like. They stayed in a cramped basement and had private tutors for the first time, because the deal meant missing a *lot* of school. On the plus side, though, only one of the girls' moms joined as a chaperone, so they had way more freedom than they'd ever had before. They didn't go wild . . . but they did do an awful lot of shopping!

We thought we were so grown-up!

Beyoncé worked harder than ever before. She was determined to make the deal work. But a few months into their gruelling schedule, they didn't seem to be making much progress, and there was no mention of a release date for their album. Then a letter came that said something like:

Dear Girls Tyme, The Dolls or whatever name you go by these days...

We've changed our minds. We think you're a bit too young and under-developed. The record deal is off.

Sorry,
Elektra Records

Are they for real!

The girls couldn't believe it. They'd come so far. They'd worked so hard! **The deal had lasted only eight months.** Beyoncé cried when she read the letter. It was *Star Search* all over again.

3   BEYONCÉ SIGNS A REAL DEAL

Mathew Knowles was not one to give up easily. He'd invested so much of his own time into Beyoncé's career, after all. The whole family had. With the news of this latest disappointment fresh in his mind, he made a big decision.

He handed in his notice at work, then told the family:

Gasp!

I'm going to manage the girls myself.

Now Beyoncé's parents were faced with some seriously tough decisions. Losing Mathew's more-than-comfortable six-figure salary put a great strain on the family finances. Mathew and Tina **sold their beautiful home** and moved into a two-bedroom apartment. They went from three cars down to one. And just when they thought things couldn't get any worse, they had to pay an unexpected tax bill. Tina was so worried about her family, she upped her hours at the salon, and for a while she even split up with Mathew.

I was devastated— had my dreams forced them apart?

Of course they hadn't . . . but Beyoncé was still only fourteen. She turned to her church to help get her through, and far from giving up her dream, she became more determined to succeed than ever.

Meanwhile, Mathew was hard at work at his new job, and the first thing he wanted was to figure out the group name. He was looking for **something with oomph** that was strong enough to get them noticed.

Tina had suggested "Destiny" a while back—the word had jumped out at her while she was reading the Bible one day—and a light had switched on for the girls. The name seemed to point to the future, as if it was their destiny to succeed. It had taken them a few months, however, to discover that about a hundred other groups had already had the same bright idea. So they decided to add the word "Child." It was kind of like a rebirth since they were starting all over again, weren't they?

Destiny's Child, yeah, that sounds good.

A BREAKTHROUGH

In 1996, after the girls had been working hard together for about five years, Destiny's Child were desperate to make the best impression. They were on their way to New York City for an audition with Teresa LaBarbera Whites, a big-shot talent scout executive from Columbia Records. Now they had a second chance at a record deal, and Destiny's Child did not want to blow it.

The girls arrived in New York and headed to Columbia Records' offices in the Sony Building hungry for success . . . but **scared out of their minds**. They auditioned in a room so small they could practically touch their audience.

There'd be no backing music either—there wasn't space for instruments. The girls had to sing a cappella.

You might think a large crowd is scary, but playing to such a small audience of really important music executives was much worse. Being so close also made it impossible to read what the execs were thinking.

> Were we nervous? Hmm, just a little!

All the girls could do now was really go for it. They performed two songs: one of their own compositions and Bill Withers's "Ain't No Sunshine." They sang their hearts out and made it to the end without any catastrophes . . . and without any real response. The executives didn't react to the performance, and the girls left their audition without having a clue what any of them thought.

Back home, **the wait was unbearable**. At times they wondered whether they'd ever hear from the record label again. Then, one day, after what seemed an eternity (but was actually only a few weeks), the girls were all hanging out at Headliners, when Tina casually handed them an envelope. It had the logo of a local diner on the front—they thought she was giving them some lunch vouchers. Beyoncé opened the envelope and let out an earsplitting whoop.

Looking over her shoulder, the girls started jumping up and down beside her.

It seemed Teresa and the other Colombia music execs had been **absolutely blown away** by their audition. They were offering Destiny's Child a contract.

For Beyoncé, it was a huge relief. She knew how much this had cost her family. Now she wanted to prove to herself that it had been worth the sacrifices.

Signing on the Dotted Line

As soon as the ink was dry on their contract, Destiny's Child hit the ground running. They had plenty of songs ready from all the months they'd spent in the studio over the past few years, and so they were able to start recording right away. It was exhausting and thrilling all at once.

In a huge stroke of luck, on July 1, 1997, their first song, "Killing Time," was released on an album for the soundtrack to *Men in Black*, starring mega-famous actor Will Smith. The film quickly became a box office hit and the soundtrack spent two weeks at number one on the *Billboard* 200. It went on to sell **three million copies** in the United States alone.

We couldn't believe it.

BILLBOARD

Billboard compiles a range of weekly US charts.

We were aiming to top both of those charts!

The Hot 100 (most popular 100 songs) and the *Billboard* 200 (most popular 200 albums) are the main ones to watch!

Now they were bona fide recording artists and people knew their name before their own album, called *Destiny's Child*, was even released. They'd finished recording most of the album by early 1997, but things move at a snail's pace in the music industry and they'd had to **wait a whole year** for it to come out. They'd actually recorded thirty-three possible tracks just to find thirteen that were **exactly right** for the album—they didn't want people to think of them as just another teenage act. They even pretended to be a few years older so they could be taken seriously.

It was worth the wait.

This being the 1990s, radio reigned supreme. Nobody listened to music on their phones or computers—people had cell phones then, but they used them, well, to call each other. When you heard a song for the first time, you most likely heard it on the radio. And that's exactly how it happened for Beyoncé and Kelly one day.

Beyoncé might have been an up-and-coming pop star, but **she still had chores** to do, and picking up her sister from school was one of them. Beyoncé and Kelly were driving in Beyoncé's brand-new Ford Explorer (the pressure on the family finances was finally easing up) when they heard some really familiar voices singing a catchy song on their favorite radio station.

The girls screeched to a halt just outside Solange's school, **pumped up the volume**, jumped out of their seats, and ran around the car screaming. When Solange walked out of school and saw them, at first she couldn't figure out what was going on. Once she realized it was Destiny's Child's "No, No, No, Part 2" blaring from the car radio (the first single from their album), she dropped her bag and joined in.

And, to top it all, **the song did well**! Really well. It probably helped that the hugely talented rapper

Wyclef Jean of the Fugees had been called in to make the song more upbeat. He sped the track up and rapped on the recording, and with his help, "No, No, No, Part 2," made it into the top ten of the *Billboard* Hot 100, eventually going platinum and selling over a million copies worldwide! The icing on the cake came later in 1998 when the song won a Soul Train Lady of Soul Award for Best R&B/Soul Single by a Group, Band, or Duo. It seemed **things were finally starting to happen** for Destiny's Child.

Being in a Band Is Hard Work

You'd think with all the false starts and uphill battles a century had passed by! But Beyoncé was still only sixteen years old when Destiny's Child's first album was released in February 1998.

If she hadn't had much downtime before, she hardly had any now. The next few months were a blur of rehearsals as the girls prepared for their first major tour. They were the opening act for Boyz II Men, the biggest boy band of the day. The boys had sold millions of albums and their mega hit "End of the Road" had broken Elvis Presley's record by staying at number one on the *Billboard* Hot 100 for *thirteen* weeks. The girls had a lot to live up to. Their dream might have come true, but **the real hard work was only just beginning**.

GOING ON TOUR, EXPLAINED

Going on tour doesn't necessarily come with all the perks y'all might expect.

We went from having all our home comforts to living on a cramped tour bus for months on end!

And since we weren't making any money when we started, when we stayed at a hotel, we had to share a room!

We had to get up early . . .

and rehearse late into the night . . .

Being so close for so much of the time meant we'd be best friends one minute and arguing the next (depending on how tired we were).

And after a while, even if you're doing something you've been waiting all your life to do, you can get really homesick.

There were also tons of press interviews. If we wanted to be taken seriously, we had to sound and act grown-up.

No one knew who we were at first, so touring with other artists and doing a ton of free radio shows helped get our name out there.

Just as they were in the thick of things, in the summer of 1998, Destiny's Child got an invitation to a birthday party—but not just any old party. This was Whitney Houston's thirty-fifth birthday!

Beyoncé and Kelly could hardly contain themselves. They *had* to go.

We scraped together what little money we had to buy matching outfits.

In fact, being out and about at music events meant the girls were rubbing shoulders with a number of the famous singers they loved, including Janet Jackson and Mariah Carey . . .

MARIAH CAREY

Born 1970
Singer, songwriter, actor

Mariah Carey's voice is famous for its incredible range: from low to high, she can span five octaves— which in singing terms is absolutely phenomenal. Beyoncé says it was after listening to Mariah that she knew she really wanted to sing. She was fascinated by "Vision of Love," Mariah's first single, released in 1990. It shot to number one in the *Billboard* Hot 100 that year. Mariah went on to have a number-one hit every year of the 1990s, with "All I Want for Christmas Is You" playing every Christmas since its release in 1994. Today she's one of the best-selling music artists of all time.

Getting Edgy

Sales of their first album might have seemed huge to the girls, but in the eyes of the big record execs the figures were average. A good start, but not a great one. The next album had to be even bigger.

In late 1998, Destiny's Child went back to the studio to work on their second album, determined to do better this time. First, they wrote down all the things they loved about their first album and all the things they didn't. **They wanted to be edgier** the second time around. They got the record label to send them an army of top producers (like She'ksperc, who was working with TLC, one of the biggest girl groups of all time)—people who could come up with the catchiest lyrics and beats. With the girls pitching in on the production and songwriting, they managed to complete the album in just a few short months.

So, in this song the girlfriend will beg her boyfriend to stay.

Oh no she won't! She would stand up to him. Let's write it like this . . .

ON AIR

Beyoncé was growing up, and she wanted to write about things that really mattered to her, especially female empowerment. *The Writing's on the Wall* was released the following year, in July 1999, and Beyoncé had cowritten and coproduced **ten of its sixteen songs**. The album was a huge success. It shot into the US charts at number six and earned a phenomenal six Grammy nominations.

The girls were sitting on top of the world, so it's hard to believe there was trouble ahead.

4   BEYONCÉ WEATHERS A STORM

Records were flying off the shelves. Throngs of fans were waiting for DC's autographs. Every time you turned the radio on (yup, radio stations still reigned supreme), it seemed their hit singles, "Bills, Bills, Bills" or "Jumpin, Jumpin," were playing. The group was quickly becoming a global sensation. Their second album went platinum in the United States . . . and Canada . . . and the UK . . . and Australia . . . and New Zealand!

Then, out of the blue, on December 14, 1999, LeToya and LaTavia **dropped a bombshell**. Rumors had been flying for years that Beyoncé and Kelly were treated better than the other two girls in the group. Mathew *was* Beyoncé's dad and he'd become the next best thing to a dad for Kelly, after all, so maybe that wouldn't be surprising—if it was true. Beyoncé and Kelly always denied that there was any favoritism, but LeToya and LaTavia saw things differently. They each sent Mathew letters to say they no longer wanted him as their manager.

Beyoncé and Kelly were devastated. They tried everything they could to keep the group together. The four girls had weekly counseling sessions with their youth minister at church. They prayed about the situation. But it just didn't work.

Beyoncé had always been the peacemaker among the four of them. She hated any drama. But now, with the group very near to collapse and all those years of hard work about to go down the toilet, she was **on the verge of a nervous breakdown**. She couldn't enjoy their success or work on writing their next big hit. She was so depressed that, at one point, she didn't leave her room for two whole weeks.

But nothing they did seemed to heal the rift between them, and soon a split seemed inevitable. For Beyoncé, it wasn't just about the group; she was losing her childhood friends. Over the last ten years, she'd shared some of the best and most memorable moments of her life with LaTavia and LeToya.

To make a painful situation even worse, Destiny's Child were on the verge of global fame, and *everyone* wanted to know their business. Once the media got wind of the story, the rumors started flying. Some people said the group had split because Beyoncé wouldn't share the limelight, while others claimed the only reason she was the lead singer was because of her dad.

In interviews, Beyoncé kept quiet about what

was going on because she didn't want to let the fans down. They all acted like everything was OK, even though it wasn't. The truth was, they hadn't been seeing eye to eye for about two years. And, at the end of the day, both sides had their own story about what caused the split.

From the outside, it looked like all of a sudden the group went from good girls with a squeaky-clean image to mean girls who dropped band members like hot potatoes.

But I always tried to put the group first!

Beyoncé felt terrible. She worried about how their fans would feel about the change in lineup, and she was upset that some of the attacks from the public felt so personal. She was also quickly learning that the media could be your friend one minute and your enemy the next. And the timing couldn't have been worse. The group were being booked everywhere to promote their new album, and their songs were getting loads of air time on the radio.

In January 2000, with two members gone, a storm of negative press, and an album to promote, Beyoncé and Kelly were carrying quite a burden, but however they were feeling, the video shoot for their next single, "Say My Name," was due to happen in just two weeks.

THE SHOW MUST GO ON

Amazingly, Beyoncé and Kelly quickly found two replacements they really liked: Michelle Williams and Farrah Franklin.

Tenitra "Michelle" Williams, born July 23, 1979, in Rockford, Illinois. Michelle sang her first solo in church at age nine. She was studying Criminal Justice at college, but left after two years to become a backup singer. Her big break was singing backing vocals for the R&B singer, Monica. She came highly recommended by one of DC's choreographers.

Farrah Destiny Franklin, born May 3, 1981, in Los Angeles, California. Originally in a band called Jane Doe, she'd met the girls when she was working as a dancer on their "Bills, Bills, Bills" video in 1999.

With very little time to get to know each other, all four girls quickly shifted gear to shoot the video on time and then waited nervously to see how the world would react . . . because Michelle and Farrah had to mime to parts that were originally sung by LaTavia and LeToya.

When it aired, the video caused a media storm. Everyone wanted to know who the two new group members were and where they came from. The girls tried their best to keep the main focus on their music, but in an unexpected twist of fate, the scandal had given the group so much publicity that they were dominating the music-industry news—and **their sales started to skyrocket**!

However, another storm was brewing. In August 2000, only five months after joining the band, Farrah left. She had her side of the story.

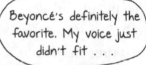

Beyoncé's definitely the favorite. My voice just didn't fit . . .

Beyoncé, Kelly, and Michelle had theirs.

The press ate it up. Nevertheless, the group moved forward with just the three members, and finally, Beyoncé felt, they had **the perfect combination**.

She never did get used to all the negative press, though. She was depressed for another two years. For the first time in her life, she had no privacy. Sometimes concertgoers gave her a hard time and people even set up hate websites writing awful stuff about her.

Before all the scandals, Beyoncé had just been a member of the group. This was never how she'd imagined her dream coming true. Maybe it was because of her mom and dad's involvement, but now, whenever something went wrong . . . the spotlight was always pointing at her.

FIGHTING BACK

But Beyoncé was ready to fight back. Later that year, Destiny's Child was on the road as the opening act on the tour of another singer who was heading for superstardom: Christina Aguilera. The girls considered themselves super lucky as they headed off to cities across the United States. Then, one morning, they tuned in to a radio talk show and heard a DJ making fun of the group's recent troubles.

Survivor was a popular reality TV show at the time, where contestants who'd been sent to live together on a remote island were gradually voted off by their teammates! Beyoncé was furious at first, but this time **she found a way to fight back**. She woke up the next day with an idea in her head, and, as they flew to their next destination on the tour, she got to work on a song called "Survivor."

The song raced to number one in the UK charts, and settled at number two in the US *Billboard* Hot 100.

But Janet Jackson had the top spot, so we didn't mind!

It wasn't just the song that made a splash; their style was important too. When the girls traveled to Jamaica to perform "Survivor," somewhere along the way, disaster struck. All their suitcases were lost and the girls arrived **without their costumes**! Creative and quick-thinking, Tina got to work. She visited the local markets, found some camouflage clothing, and started cutting!

We had a new set of costumes and we were right on trend!

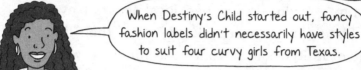

When Destiny's Child started out, fancy fashion labels didn't necessarily have styles to suit four curvy girls from Texas.

I'll make sure you girls have some spectacular costumes!

We couldn't afford designer dresses most of the time anyway. So, in the early days—inspired by the amazing outfits the Supremes and other girl groups wore in the 1960s—Mom started to make most of our costumes herself.

Wearing my mom's designs made me feel strong, proud, and invincible —like a warrior and a queen.

She sewed hundreds of crystals and pearls onto our first costumes, putting so much passion and love into every small detail.

And, just like that, she became Destiny's Child's stylist. Before long her designs would be recognized around the world.

61

INDEPENDENT WOMEN

Destiny's Child already had loyal fans all over the world, and in October 2000, they had their first real taste of Hollywood. Beyoncé was nineteen when the group's "Independent Women, Part 1" was chosen as the opening song on the soundtrack of the international hit movie, *Charlie's Angels*. She was ecstatic, especially since she'd cowritten it. The song was a salute to all the independent women around the world who work hard, live their dreams, and take care of themselves.

> I wanted young women to know that you *can* pay your own bills, you *can* do things your way, and you *don't* have to depend on anyone.

Having a song in another blockbluster film was incredible exposure for the girls. This time, though, they got to make a flashy music video that included cameo appearances from the stars: Cameron Diaz, Lucy Liu, and Drew Barrymore. Then the song had massive airplay all over the world—in the UK, Canada, and as far away as Japan. **They had a hit on their hands.** The song shot straight to number one on the *Billboard*

Hot 100 and stayed there for *eleven* consecutive weeks! "Independent Women, Part 1" was such a chartbuster that it gained an entry in the *Guinness World Records 2001* for "longest-running number one song by a female group."

Oh, What a Night!

On February 21, 2001, the girls were running late for the Grammys—the biggest music awards ceremony the music industry has to offer. They quickly ticked off their glam checklist, which didn't just include fancy hair and makeup: they'd splurged on some Versace outfits! The girls had the very great honor of performing at that year's ceremony!

Destiny's Child had also been nominated for an astonishing **five Grammy awards** (they'd had nominations before but hadn't ever won). They were about to bolt out of their hotel room when their publicist burst in, saying: "You won! You won Best R&B Song!" She had a huge smile on her face.

The girls stared back in shock. They were ecstatic, of course, but their minds were focused on the ceremony, so there was no time to celebrate—they were about to make the performance of their lives.

They were the follow-up act to legendary singer-songwriter Madonna, who would be watching their performance from the front row of the star-studded audience.

Beyoncé was especially in awe of Madonna. She'd always admired how the megastar managed to rewrite the music industry rules.

MADONNA

Born 1958
Singer, songwriter, dancer, actress

One of the big pop legends of the 1980s and 1990s, Madonna is also known for stirring things up (like when she danced in front of burning crosses in her "Like a Prayer" video). The music industry is generally run by men, but Madonna never let anyone stand in her way—Beyoncé loved her for that, because she didn't believe in barriers either. Madonna created her own opportunities and became one of the best-selling female artists of all time!

To get to the stage, there was a spiral staircase to negotiate. The girls made it to the bottom without a mishap, stiletto heels pinching their feet. Phew! Then the three of them held hands and offered up a quick prayer. Suddenly, the auditorium flooded with light and there they were, with a huge video screen behind them, and the **who's who of music royalty sprawled** out in front of them.

This was Destiny's Child's biggest gig to date, and they were ready to show the world of music exactly what they were capable of. A booming voice announced the performance, and Beyoncé suddenly became calm just as she had way back when she was seven years old! The music started and the girls **lit up the stage** with their performance.

Singing "Independent Women, Part 1," they were all set to segue into "Say My Name," when Michelle had a mishap. She was supposed to do a simple costume change: pulling off the legs of her pants to transform them into shorts. But when one trouser leg got caught on her boot, **she missed her cue**. It was looking like Kelly and Beyoncé would have to finish the set without her. They hadn't prepared for anything like this.

Thank goodness Tina was backstage to lend a hand, calm nerves, and fix wayward costumes as usual. She snapped the pants off like a magician and sent Michelle back onstage! Luckily, nobody caught on and the girls finished their set to a **standing ovation** that sounded like rolling thunder.

With the nerve-racking part of the evening over, the girls could settle down to focus on the awards, but not long after they'd taken their seats they were standing up again—their names had been called. They'd won a second Grammy! They could hardly believe it.

Here's how they did overall:

☆ ☆ **The Grammy Awards for 2000** ☆ ☆

"Independent Women"	Best Song Written for a Motion Picture, Television or Other Visual Media	(Nominated)
"Say My Name"	Record of the Year	(Nominated)
"Say My Name"	Song of the Year	(Nominated)
"Say My Name"	Best R&B Song	(Won)
"Say My Name"	Best R&B Performance by a Duo or Group with Vocals	(Won)

Could the night get any better? Believe it or not, it could, because the girls had invitations to a ton of after-parties. Beyoncé met some of her **absolute idols**, like Gloria Estefan and Shakira! Then, at the Sony after-party, they came **face-to-face with Sir Elton John**. He kissed each girl on the cheek . . . and invited them along to another party!

5 BEYONCÉ SPREADS HER WINGS

In April 2001, in Omaha, Nebraska, **an auditorium was buzzing**. The kids at Millard North High School were waiting in the gym for the school assembly to start. Some were overwhelmed. Others were jumping up and down with excitement. A while back, the kids had won a radio contest by scrabbling together 1.6 million pennies (or $16,000) for underprivileged children. The prize: a visit from Destiny's Child. The school performance had been booked before the songs "Independent Women, Part 1" and "Survivor" became global sensations.

But now Destiny's Child were megastars with a third album about to be released, and the kids of Millard North couldn't contain themselves.

Destiny's Child took to the stage with their shiny outfits and their backup dancers in tow. It was like they'd been beamed down from another planet. Awestruck, the kids calmed down. Handmade "YOU RULE" signs were slowly lowered and the show began.

Beyoncé's ponytail whipped around like a golden rope as she sang. The girls belted out their hits just as they would at any other concert. **The kids were transfixed.** At the end of the forty-five-minute show, the trio and their entourage cleared out of the gym as fast as they came in and settled into their fancy tour bus.

A Surprise Call

So many good things were happening for nineteen-year-old Beyoncé. Destiny's Child were on a roll. And when their third album, also called *Survivor*, came out, it shot straight to the number one spot on the *Billboard* 200 chart in May 2001. This sent a clear message: Destiny's Child was here to stay.

The phone was ringing off the hook with endorsement offers:

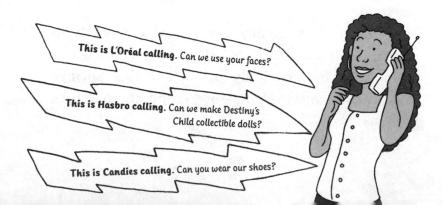

This is L'Oréal calling. Can we use your faces?

This is Hasbro calling. Can we make Destiny's Child collectible dolls?

This is Candies calling. Can you wear our shoes?

And then Beyoncé got a call that she *really* wasn't expecting.

MTV rang! They wanted her to take the lead role in a film they were making for their TV channel. *Carmen: The Hip Hopera* was an updated version of a 125-year-old classical opera. Beyoncé was flabbergasted . . . and flattered! But Carmen was a bold, devious, and manipulative character, and Beyoncé worried that acting the part might affect her wholesome image and upset some of the fans. At the same time, though, **she was itching to give acting a go**, and anyway, why couldn't she be a singer, songwriter, dancer, producer, *and* actor?

> I wanted to work hard to show the music industry and the world that you can be down-to-earth, sensitive, AND successful.

She worked hard to learn as much as she could about her role and tried to prepare herself for twelve weeks on set (that's how long they had to film the movie).

It was a big step. Beyoncé missed her family so much. It felt like she'd been sleeping in a bed across from Kelly for practically her whole life. Solange was always somewhere nearby blaring out loud rock music. Now, suddenly, Beyoncé was on her own: her dad wasn't around to make all her business decisions, and her mom couldn't wake her up with scrambled eggs in the morning.

Although it helped that the movie was more or less a musical and she could rap and sing, there were still plenty of uncomfortable things. Beyoncé had been **dreading the kissing scene** from the minute she'd found out about it.

Just pretend you're kissing a boyfriend.

What boyfriend?

Beyoncé hadn't had too many of those. She and her first boyfriend, Lyndall Locke, had recently broken up. They'd dated for about six years and Beyoncé even went to his prom. But once she'd started recording and performing, dating became difficult. She hadn't been able to see Lyndall that much, and they eventually broke up.

Beyoncé had recently started hanging out with superstar rapper and music producer Shawn Corey Carter, aka Jay-Z, but it was **all very hush-hush**. As far as anyone knew, they were just good friends. So picturing a boyfriend for her first on-screen kiss wasn't exactly going to work.

When the day came to film the scene, Beyoncé was so nervous, but she knew how to prepare herself for a show. And that's what she did. It took a few takes, but watching the movie, no one would have guessed how she was really feeling!

And on the plus side, working on the set of *Carmen*, Beyoncé could actually let her guard down and make some new friends.

As strange as it sounds, I was just now learning how to talk to new people.

By the end of those twelve weeks, Beyoncé's self-esteem and self-confidence had really improved.

HEADLINERS

As soon as *Carmen* wrapped in early 2001, Beyoncé and the girls packed their bags and sped across the country—straight into the mayhem and excitement of their very first headlining tour. After years of being an opening act for other big artists, **Destiny's Child was finally the main attraction**.

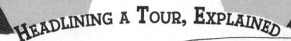

Now that we were bigger stars, we had bigger everything. Our tour buses were more luxurious . . .

Our live shows had more WOW factor!

We wanted pyro, stages coming out of the floor . . . the whole nine yards.

We upped the glam factor too.

Mom was still making most of our costumes, but we wanted to wear some of the big-name fashion designers like Versace and Christian Dior too.

We didn't have to share dressing rooms or hotel rooms. On our very first tour with Boyz II Men, we didn't even have a closet to change in. Now we got to make special requests . . .

Destiny's Child Backstage Perks

☆ Six bottles of Snapple Iced Tea

☆ Soda, chips and salsa, a fresh fruit tray, and a deli tray (no pork)

☆ Lemons, honey, and fresh ginger

☆ Fresh flowers

☆ Strawberry-scented candles

☆ Real china and cutlery (no plastic)

TRAGEDY!

Just as Destiny's Child were preparing for the European leg of their world tour, **something terrible happened**. On September 11, 2001, four hijacked planes carried out terrorist attacks in New York City, Washington, DC, and Philadelphia, sending shockwaves around the world and killing almost 3,000 people. The girls were in Los Angeles for the Latin Grammy Awards when they found out . . . and they were terrified. Mathew was in New York at the time, and other members of the girls' team had loved ones there. The Knowles family was scattered across the country, and Beyoncé couldn't wait for them all to get home to Houston so they could be together.

A few weeks later, in October, the girls nervously stepped on a plane to travel to New York and then Washington, DC. They'd agreed to perform at two benefit concerts for the victims of the 9/11 attacks. Without the backing dancers they'd had on tour and not having practiced it in a while, the group wasn't planning to perform "Survivor" at either gig, but after the New York concert, Mathew persuaded them. "You know how many people out there feel like survivors and need to hear that song?" he said. The girls could only agree.

In such uncertain times, the girls didn't want to be

on the road, so they postponed their overseas travels and focused on projects closer to home.

SECOND ACT

With the unexpected gap in her touring schedule, Beyoncé auditioned for another acting role, a comedy this time. She didn't really expect to get it, especially because, after the producer had asked her how she felt about doing comedy, she'd answered:

Oops! Sometimes being blunt isn't the best option, and this time Beyoncé really **thought she'd blown it**, so imagine her surprise when she found out she'd actually got the part. Next thing she knew, in the fall of 2001, she was on her way to Hollywood to film the big-budget blockbuster and spoof spy movie, *Goldmember*, the third film in the Austin Powers series. Playing

Powers' sidekick, the funny and feisty undercover spy Foxxy Cleopatra, Beyoncé found herself punching, kicking, and slapping, while dressed in gold and wearing an enormous afro wig.

KAPOW!

Oof!

Beyoncé worked extra hard to be taken seriously by the full-time actors on set (she was still only twenty, remember!). And it worked. People really liked her performance, and she even got nominated for a Teen Choice Award for "Breakout Female Movie Star."

Beyoncé had been bitten by the acting bug, and tons of acting offers soon came rolling in, but she still had to focus on her singing. Several months after 9/11, the girls finally felt it was safe enough to travel. So, in the spring of 2002, Beyoncé and Destiny's Child were on the road again, kicking off their tour with a gig at home in Houston, then heading for Australia, Japan, Belgium, France, Germany, Scandinavia, Holland, and the UK!

The girls put on an **absolutely awesome show**. They had a five-piece band, ten back-up dancers, and plenty of fireworks. With fire and flair, **they blew their fans away**, performing all their biggest hits.

But even during this exciting whirl around the world, Beyoncé was still Beyoncé and wanted to keep things familiar.

My family is always a part of what I do . . . even a world Tour!

It must have helped to have her family around, especially because Beyoncé and the girls were always hard at work on these long tours. They performed six days a week and—with all the shows, interviews, and appearances—there was no end in sight.

One day, in June 2002, the girls found themselves in London. They'd just released their autobiography, *Soul Survivors*, in the middle of the tour and had to get up two hours early for a book signing in the famous department store, Selfridges. OK, so they did squeeze some shopping in as well—they were in London after all! Then they jumped into their chauffeured SUV and went to prepare for a show at Wembley Stadium.

Solange had been with the group as a backing dancer for a while, and now she got her moment in the spotlight, taking on the role of compère to welcome the girls onto the Wembley stage.

The group hopped onstage and wowed the crowd with a larger-than-life performance that lasted a full hour and a half.

Straight after their closing number, Beyoncé's dad called everyone—including all the dancers and crew—backstage for an emergency meeting. There hadn't been any major hiccups with the show. What could be wrong?

Then Solange walked in, and everyone broke into a loud and cheery rendition of "Happy Birthday." She'd danced, sung, and now she was compèring for the band, and she was **only just turning sixteen**! Solange blew out the candles on her chocolate cake and started dancing in a circle. Everyone jumped in, even Mathew.

GOODBYE GIRLS

Beyoncé loved performing with Destiny's Child and the three girls were all the best of friends, but she'd had a taste of independence, and when the tour ended in 2002 they all made a major decision: they would **take a three-year break** so they could each do their own thing.

The announcement caused a media sensation, and again the press tried to make out that the girls had had a falling-out. The future of the group seemed up in the air. But Destiny's Child were just exhausted! They'd worked really hard for three whole years and now they really needed to take a break.

Just before this, in May 2002, while they were still on tour, Beyoncé got some amazing news. The American Society of Composers, Authors and Publishers' (ASCAP) Pop Music Awards was naming her Songwriter of the Year for three songs: "Independent Women, Part 1," "Jumpin, Jumpin," and "Survivor." It was much more than just another notch on her belt. In fact, it was the perfect confidence boost for her next project.

I was only the second woman and the first Black woman to win it—ever! And there have been so many great female songwriters. Well, I was happy to help bust the door open for other female artists.

6　BEYONCÉ GOES SOLO

Now that she was taking a break, Beyoncé could have spent all the time in the world doing some of the things she loved, such as painting and listening to her old-time favorites, like Aretha Franklin and James Brown. Or she could have parked herself at home in Houston to hang out with family and catch a few services at her local church. But this was Beyoncé—no way would she be lying low for long.

THE HEAT IS ON

There was a great weight of expectation on her, but Beyoncé wanted to take her time and experiment with something new. And although Mathew was still her manager, she wanted to handle as much as she could herself. So when she started work on her solo album in 2002, she had **a pretty good idea** of the process she needed to follow; after all, she'd been working with producers since she was twelve years old.

☆ She holed up in a Miami
hotel for months
to write new material.

I wanted to be by the ocean!

☆ Instead of going to see music producers, she got them to come to her, contacting every single well-known US producer from Missy Elliott to Scott Storch.

☆ In a two-day marathon session, she gave each one a thirty-minute slot to pitch their ideas.

When Beyoncé interviewed Rich Harrison, he told her he'd had a sample—a recording of part of an old 1970s song called "Are You My Woman? (Tell Me So)"—running around his head for some time. He'd played it for his friends. None of them liked it, but as far as Rich was concerned, that was good news. It meant the style was different, and **different was just what Beyoncé was looking for**. She didn't like his idea right away, though. She thought it sounded too retro, but then she had an idea:

When Beyoncé returned, two hours later, Rich had managed to compose some verses to tell the story of the song and he'd been working on a hook—a catchy little phrase that repeats throughout the song. Beyoncé liked what he'd done, but something was still missing. As they brainstormed ideas, Beyoncé caught sight of her self in the mirror and noticed that her hair was all over the place and her clothes didn't match:

Beyoncé added the "uh-oh" line to give the song its bridge—that's the middle part that keeps the listener's interest. When it came to the recording, Rich played all the instruments on the track himself.

Someone else had been quietly helping out behind the scenes, and the night before Rich finished the album, **Jay-Z added an extra touch of him rapping**. "Crazy in Love" was ready to roll.

The song was released in May 2003. This was Beyoncé's first solo single and the lead song on her first solo album, *Dangerously in Love*. Columbia Records wasn't sure about it. In fact, they weren't sold on Beyoncé's whole album. After all her hard work recording forty-three songs to find the fifteen tracks that made it onto the album, there was talk that the label might not even release it because they **didn't think it had a single hit on it**.

How wrong they were! The album went platinum three weeks after it was released and sold 11 million copies around the world. The company was right about one thing, though.

I didn't have just one hit song on that album—I had five!

"Crazy in Love" went on to win loads of awards!

THE DOWNSIDE OF FAME

With Jay-Z working on the album, rumors about a possible relationship between the two reached fever pitch once it was released. It even sounded like some of the songs might be about him. Beyoncé didn't confirm the relationship. But she didn't deny it either. She didn't like to talk about her private life.

But now that Beyoncé was a solo star, it was like she was under a microscope. Her life wasn't her own anymore. **She absolutely loved her fans** and always wanted to do her best for them, but sometimes the demands of public life could be overwhelming. Everywhere she went, people wanted to meet her.

I'm still just a regular human being. And I miss doing everyday things . . . like running to the supermarket to buy toilet paper.

. . . or grabbing an ice-cream cone . . . or watching a movie in an actual movie theater . . .

And if she couldn't hide her face in public, she certainly couldn't hide when things went wrong. On the opening night of her first solo tour on November 3, 2003, everything was set up: the bright lights, the clouds of smoke, the fireworks—but the show didn't quite go according to plan:

☆ Her tour manager fell off the stage and injured his back.

☆ Her opening number was delayed for over an hour, so tired kids in the audience were crying before Beyoncé came on.

☆ When she finally did appear, lowered head-first from the ceiling by a trapeze-like contraption, there was a problem with the wiring and she had to stop mid-song.

☆ Then her costume changes took too long!

It was a mess, and Beyoncé wasn't exactly the wonder onstage that she'd hoped to be. Needless to say, the reviews weren't so great. But **this was part of the job**. She didn't let it get her down; she took every failure as a chance to improve, and within a few days things were running like clockwork. Plus, she had secret backstage support from an unexpected source: Jay-Z. And the papers didn't know a thing about it.

It's good to keep some things private.

SASHA FIERCE

Beyoncé had developed a technique for handling the enormous pressure of performing. Remember the stage fright she'd had as a kid? Well, it had followed her from the little stage to the BIGGEST ones! Earlier in the year (May 2003), she'd been singing and dancing her heart out totally engrossed in her performance when something came over her and she threw a **$250,000 pair of earrings** into the crowd without thinking.

After the show, her cousin and assistant, Angie, had the impossible job of trying to find the suddenly rich fan who'd caught the earrings to demand they hand them back. Meanwhile, Beyoncé was puzzled. She couldn't explain why she'd thrown the earrings. She was so fearless onstage that night, it was as if **someone else had taken over**. She decided to name that part of herself Sasha Fierce. And her onstage alter ego was born.

Sasha would prove to be super helpful. She took over when Beyoncé's wisdom teeth were giving her grief just before a show in France, when she needed to forget the pain and perform her heart out. She showed up when Beyoncé floated down from the rafters to perform her solo debut of "Crazy in Love" and "Baby Boy" at the 2003 MTV Video Music Awards. And Sasha really showed up at two extremely nerve-racking performances just one week apart in early 2004 . . .

SHOWSTOPPERS

The year had started with a bang for Beyoncé. First, she'd fulfilled her childhood dream by **singing the national anthem** at Super Bowl XXXVIII on February 1. Houston was hosting the Super Bowl that year, and singing in front of her hometown crowd made it even more special. Over 100 million people were watching on TV as she got on the stage. The performance was a huge success, but there was no time to bask in glory . . .

The Grammy nominations quickly followed, and she was up for six awards for *Dangerously in Love*. She'd already agreed to perform at that year's show. But Ken Ehrlich, Grammy producer extraordinaire, wanted to make a show that would go down in Grammy history—an unforgettable performance with two great singers: one a legend, the other a rising star.

Ken had already sensed interest from Prince—the "legend" of the duo. Now he just needed "rising star"

Beyoncé to agree. But when he asked her, she didn't jump in with an immediate yes. Ken was puzzled.

PRINCE

1958–2016
Singer, songwriter

Prince was a huge star in the 1980s and one of Beyoncé's all-time favorite musicians. He wrote amazing songs and played dozens of instruments. He also had style—often sporting flamboyant suits atop his trademark heeled boots. With huge hits that included "Purple Rain," "When Doves Cry," and "1999," he was easily one of the best American musicians of his generation.

Ken finally got Beyoncé to agree to the duet, on one condition: she wanted to sing her own song too. She'd been working toward this opportunity all her life; it would be her first solo performance at the Grammys, and **she wanted to make her mark**.

By the time they met to rehearse, one week before the show, Prince, being the genius performer and brilliant musician that he was, had already worked out their entire routine. Beyoncé was starstruck and absolutely petrified. All she could do was hope she wouldn't mess up!

And she didn't. On February 8, 2004, Prince took to the stage first, wearing a purple suit with a gold shirt and tie, and Beyoncé followed in a sparkly shocking pink dress. They performed a four-song medley to open the Grammys and gave one of the **greatest performances in the show's history**!

If that wasn't enough to stop the show, Beyoncé's solo performance surely was. Wearing a long, glittery, turquoise and silver gown, she sang "Dangerously in Love 2" on a stage that had been transformed into a huge gold picture frame (with seventeen backing singers, dancers, and musicians). As the song ended, a white dove flew down from the rafters and effortlessly landed in the palm of her hand.

Beyoncé went on to win *five* of those six awards she'd been nominated for. What a night!

DRESSING UP

So many Destiny's Child fans had asked how they could follow the group's style, and even more had been clamoring to dress like Beyoncé since she'd become a successful solo artist, that it had gotten Beyoncé thinking. She wanted to create a clothing line that would appeal to young girls.

House of Deréon was first announced in September 2004. Named after Beyoncé's seamstress grandmother, Agnèz Deréon, it **immediately made a splash**, even featuring on the Oprah Winfrey Show. The brand's tagline was "Couture. Kick. Soul." It was inspired by three generations of women: Beyoncé's mom (the couture), Beyoncé (the kick), and her grandma (the soul). It mixed hip-hop influences with more grown-up elegance.

☆ Cocktail and evening dresses inspired by Beyoncé's red-carpet looks.

☆ Lots of denim hip-hop style for younger fans.

☆ A plus-sized collection called Curvelicious for more shapely ladies.

The brand made it into a lot of well-known department stores, including Macy's and Bloomingdale's, but it didn't turn into the success Beyoncé and Tina had hoped for.

Beyoncé's influence on fashion hasn't stopped, though. She's set a lot of trends along the way. From supersized statement earrings to sparkly, sequinned mini-dresses and figure-hugging gowns that show off her curves, she's always followed her own style (with a bit of help from her mom).

But every now and then, I still love a good ol' pair of denim cut-off shorts and a plain white T-shirt.

7   BEYONCÉ'S DATE WITH DESTINY

The three-year break was nearly at an end, and Beyoncé had managed to accomplish all her goals— and she was still only twenty-three! She'd proven herself as a singer and an actor. She'd won multiple awards and broken records, both with the group and as a solo artist. She'd written songs that people responded to and she'd had fun doing it.

Meanwhile, Kelly and Michelle had been busy too. Michelle had made a gospel album, *Heart to Yours*, that reached number one on the *Billboard* Gospel Albums chart. And Kelly had worked with the happening hip-hop artist Nelly on a song called "Dilemma," which was a huge hit—she even won a Grammy for it—before releasing her own solo album, *Simply Deep*.

The girls had been each other's number-one fans, and now they were **ready to share the stage again**. In November 2004, their fourth album, *Destiny Fulfilled*, hit the shelves as the girls were preparing for a world tour.

THE FINAL HURRAH

The new show was massive, touring more than seventy cities, from Hiroshima to New York City, and the girls spared no detail, mesmerizing the crowds wherever they went.

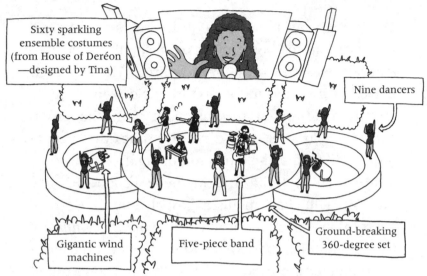

Sixty sparkling ensemble costumes (from House of Deréon —designed by Tina)

Nine dancers

Gigantic wind machines

Five-piece band

Ground-breaking 360-degree set

The show in Vancouver, Canada, on September 10, 2005, was their very last stop. The air buzzed with electricity. As the girls belted out their hits, "Say My Name," "Independent Women," and "Bills, Bills, Bills," cameras flashed and the arena rumbled with cheers from thousands of fans.

Beyoncé and Kelly had been **singing together for fifteen years**. They'd sung as a threesome with Michelle for five of those years. They clearly had chemistry and they were having a blast onstage. The audience clapped and cheered and sang along with every word. It must have been overwhelming . . . and gratifying. They'd worked so hard to make it this far.

The girls each sang their solo hits, and when it was Beyoncé's turn to sing "Baby Boy" and "Naughty Girl," the crowd erupted. It was a bittersweet moment. As the end of the show approached, she was uncharacteristically emotional. During her solo performance of "Dangerously in Love," there were tears in her eyes.

Usually, Beyoncé wasn't one to cry in public, nevermind in front of an audience of thousands of cheering fans, but tonight she wasn't just saying goodbye to the tour, she was saying goodbye to the group. The girls had agreed this would be **their last-ever tour**, and tonight, their last-ever performance together. They might still sing with each other in the future, but not as Destiny's Child. They'd had an unbelievable time and achieved success way beyond their wildest dreams, but now they were ready to move on.

After their final encore, Beyoncé, Kelly, and Michelle hugged each other for a long time. Then they turned to the audience with linked arms, bowed, and said goodnight.

The Role of a Lifetime

The tour was over, and she'd said goodbye to her best friends, so you'd think it was finally time for a break. But when Beyoncé came across the script for a movie called *Dreamgirls*, any plans she might've had to slow down were thrown out of the window. **She'd been waiting for a chance like this**.

The movie was a remake of a Broadway musical about a group of African American singers—Deena, Effie, and Lorrell—who made their way up the pop charts in the 1960s. It was inspired by Diana Ross and the Supremes. Beyoncé had listened to the Supremes as she was growing up, and she'd seen *Dreamgirls* on Broadway and loved the musical since she was sixteen. She desperately wanted to play Deena, who wasn't even the star of the show, and thought the part would help her to develop as an actress.

But the film's director, Bill Condon, wasn't so sure. He worried that Beyoncé was too big a celebrity to pull it off. He couldn't have known that transforming into someone else was exactly what Beyoncé wanted right then.

Determined to prove to him that she really could be Deena, Beyoncé flew in her makeup artists and stylist to help her get the look just right for the audition. This meant:

☆ Finding a seriously ugly vintage dress (Deena had terrible taste when she was young!).

☆ Wearing an unbelievably awful wig.

☆ And working with an acting coach so she could turn on the tears at the drop of a hat.

The next day, Beyoncé got a call. **The role was hers**. Now she really threw herself into the part, studying performances by Diana Ross and the Supremes to get the postures just right and covering the walls of her trailer with pictures of the group.

Dreamgirls got a ton of good reviews. It was nominated for eight Academy Awards and won two of them. There were no awards for Beyoncé this time, but people had definitely noticed her and seen how hard she had worked.

I'd shown the world I wasn't just a pop diva, and I'd loved it so much I would have done the part for free.

Back in the Studio

Outside of work, Beyoncé's life was pretty low-key. She kept the same, very small, close-knit circle around her. Mathew was still her manager. Tina still made her costumes. Kelly and Michelle were still her best friends. Solange and her cousin, Angie, helped her write songs. Jay-Z, whom she'd "officially" been dating for about a year now, was always around too.

And just days after she finished filming *Dreamgirls*, Beyoncé was back in the studio, **buzzing with ideas**. She wanted to pour all of the dramatic energy from her role as Deena into an album that spoke for all women. She got to work lightning fast. Here's how the process happened this time around:

☆ Beyoncé booked the biggest and the best R&B/hip-hop producers in the world (again)—Rich Harrison, Rodney "Darkchild" Jerkins, Swizz Beatz, and Sean Garrett.

☆ She rented out FOUR recording studios at the same time and gave each producer a room to work in.

☆ She moved between studios to see how her producers were doing.

No pressure, but Rodney came up with a stellar beat next door. You got any ideas yet?

Er . . .

☆ When Beyoncé had an idea for a song, she'd share it with her producers. She and one team would come up with the lyrics. Another team would work up the music. And in just three hours the song would be made!

☆ Solange and Angie were always on hand to help with song-writing. They ordered fast food between sessions and kept Beyoncé dancing when she wasn't writing.

After about three weeks of fourteen-hour work days, Beyoncé and her team had made an entire album. And on September 5, 2006, one day after her twenty-fifth birthday, *B'Day* was released in the United States. She'd just given herself the coolest birthday present ever!

The fans gave me an even better one. *B'Day* sold half a million copies in seven days!

All the while, Beyoncé had been doing something she'd never done before in her entire career. She'd been **working without telling her dad**. She was a grown-up now; she didn't always have to do things Mathew's way. Besides, it wasn't just her dad who didn't know about the album—she hadn't really told anyone else either. Well, except for Angie . . . and Solange . . . and Jay-Z.

An Unusual Call

By now, Beyoncé knew the drill: you release an album, you prepare for another globe-trotting tour. But this time, she wanted to do things differently. So, she put out an unusual call. She wanted a rocking ten-piece live band onstage with her . . . but **it had to be all-female**! She really took female empowerment to heart.

From Tokyo to Texas, women heard the call and flocked to the auditions. Needless to say, the competition was stiff (a lot of the women were classically trained) . . . and the process was grueling. Beyoncé took three days to audition hundreds of women. Once she had narrowed it down, she had the two most talented women on each instrument battle for the top spot and Mathew was on hand to help her pick the best of each pair.

May the fiercest woman win!

With the band all figured out, Beyoncé packed her bags and headed out with her team. And there were a lot of them! Her enormous entourage included:

- ☆ The all-female ten-piece band, called Suga Mama.
- ☆ Three female backing singers.
- ☆ Ten dancers (six women and four men).
- ☆ Seventy-five stage and crew members.
- ☆ Sixty tons of stage equipment, most of it lighting.

The tour sold out.

A SECRET

The press had speculated about Beyoncé and Jay-Z's relationship for years now. Was it on? Was it off? Had they married in December 2007? The couple kept their cards close to their chest.

And then, on April 4, 2008, in a top-secret, super-intimate ceremony, the pair finally did become Mr. and Mrs. Carter. Beyoncé hadn't wanted a big wedding. Her dress was simple, made by Tina, of course, though Jay-Z did give her a **five-million-dollar ring**. There were no photographs allowed.

And, boy, did they have a blast! The party lasted until 5 a.m., and with only around forty guests it was months before the press found out.

A Ring

Beyoncé might not have wanted to talk about her marriage publicly, but her real life always managed to find a way into her music.

Just a month after her wedding, in May 2008, singer-songwriter The-Dream had an idea. They were working together on Beyoncé's third album, *I Am . . . Sasha Fierce*. Dream noticed Beyoncé wasn't wearing her very expensive ring and had a thought: lots of women are waiting for their boyfriends to propose . . . they should write about that. Beyoncé agreed, and with the help of a few other songwriters, the two of them wrote up some lyrics and made a recording. They called the song "Single Ladies (Put a Ring on It)."

Beyoncé didn't throw a lot of money or time into a video for the song—no hair or wardrobe changes, no elaborate set. It was just Beyoncé and two backing dancers. It **took only twelve hours** to get the whole thing right. And then "Single Ladies" took on a life of its own. The song:

☆ Had over four million digital downloads.

☆ Won three Grammys.

☆ Became Beyoncé's highest-selling hit.

☆ Inspired a global dance craze.

On top of all that, it got its own comedy sketch on the TV show *Saturday Night Live*—**a sure sign of success**! Singer Justin Timberlake was a regular guest on the show, and after turning up at the door of Beyoncé's dressing room one day, wearing a black leotard, he tried to persuade her that he (and some comedian friends) should perform the dance on the show with her. Beyoncé couldn't help but laugh—and she accepted the challenge.

8 BEYONCÉ SHATTERS GLASS

Beyoncé had always wanted to be her own boss. After all, she'd watched both her parents running their own businesses while she was growing up. And if someone was going to make money from all her hard work, it made sense it should be Beyoncé. She was world-famous, and she'd made millions of dollars. She had the power, and the money, to do what she wanted. So, in 2008, at twenty-seven, **she set up her own company** in New York. She named it Parkwood Entertainment after the street she grew up on in Houston and made herself its CEO (chief executive officer). Mathew was still in the picture, but now the buck definitely stopped and started with Beyoncé.

I wanted to shatter that glass ceiling in the music industry and show other women that you could be successful and you could do it your own way.

And since Parkwood had an agreement with Beyoncé's longtime record label, Sony Music's Columbia Records, she could still afford to go big with her music. For her albums, Parkwood and Columbia split the costs of making, distributing, and marketing the music—and they split the profit—but Parkwood took total charge of the creative side, like choosing which music producers to work with. It was **the best of both worlds** for Beyoncé.

With her cousin Angie as vice president of operations, Parkwood started out small, making Beyoncé's videos and films, but went on to do loads more in fashion (a collaboration with Topshop creating athletic wear) and the arts (signing other teen music artists). So, is artist Beyoncé different from CEO Beyoncé? Well, not much.

1. Beyoncé's not the kind of CEO who sits around in her office all day. She likes to walk around from one office to the next.

2. She still likes teamwork—hearing what people have to say and what projects they are working on.

3. She likes to challenge other people and she likes to be challenged.

Nothing's impossible, right?

4. Beyoncé works hard in the office, often eighteen hours a day!

She soon put her young business to the test. Beyoncé had a new song ("Halo"), a new movie coproduced by Parkwood (*Obsessed*), a new world tour (I Am . . .), a new spring clothing collection . . . you get the picture. Let's have a look at her New York City schedule for one week in late April 2009.

Schedule April 2009

Monday: Ten-hour modeling session for House of Deréon fashion lines.

Tuesday: Music video shoot for new song, 10 a.m. till 2 a.m. Wednesday morning.

Wednesday: First of thirty-six TV and radio interviews to promote new movie, *Obsessed*.

Thursday: First screening of *Obsessed*—hundreds of cheering fans turn out to say hi.

Friday: Four talk-show appearances and one live performance.

Saturday: Packing for tomorrow's trip.

Sunday: Off to Croatia to kick off the 110-date I Am . . . World Tour.

By now, Beyoncé had sold millions of records, won a handful of Grammys (in 2010, she'd go on to win six in one night, the most for a female artist in the Grammys' fifty-two-year history), acted in seven films, and headlined three solo tours. She'd also made a boatload of money: **roughly $87 million** in 2009 alone.

By early 2010, Beyoncé had been working practically **nonstop for thirteen years**.

TIME FOR A BREAK

While her career had been going great, Beyoncé's personal life wasn't so hot. Her parents had split up—for good this time—and she was at a crossroads about her father's role in her career. She wanted the pressure to ease off for once, so remember that break she'd been thinking about since, oh, for ever? Well, now she really did take it.

She took almost a year off and spent much of it doing everyday things, like cooking for Jay-Z and sleeping in her own bed. She went to gigs as a member of the audience. She toured with Jay-Z, watching him from in front of the stage for the first time.

He's not bad!

She went to museums and the ballet and did a lot of things that many people only dream of, like visiting the Great Wall of China and the pyramids in Egypt.

Then, at the end of 2010, it was time to face the music again!

A GUT-WRENCHING DECISION

The break had been good for Beyoncé. She was fired up with inspiration and ready to get back to business. It wasn't long before she was **making headlines**. On March 28, 2011, Beyoncé made an official announcement that left friends and fans reeling. She had fired her manager. It was the end of the road for her professional relationship with Mathew.

The whole experience was devastating. He'd been managing Beyoncé's career for nearly eighteen years.

But I'm your dad, you can't fire me!

I'm not firing you as my dad, I'm firing you as my manager.

He'd sacrificed his job and home and now, with his marriage over too, it must have felt as though the family was falling apart. It can't have been easy for Beyoncé, but she knew it was the right decision for her career, for her business, and for her independence as a woman.

It was time to move on.

SOMETHING BLUE

In August 2011, Beyoncé was performing at the MTV Video Music Awards. She really liked to surprise her audiences, and this time she had an absolute showstopper. During her performance, she cradled her stomach and asked the audience to feel the love that was growing inside her. The world went crazy. Beyoncé and Jay-Z were **having a baby**!

Five months later, on January 7, 2012, a bouncing baby girl, Blue Ivy Carter, was quietly welcomed into the world. As usual, the press were not invited, and to make sure no photos were leaked, it's said Jay-Z and Beyoncé paid the hospital a **million dollars** to hire an entire floor of its building. They didn't want pictures of their baby girl leaking to the press.

Blue Ivy's life needed to be as normal as possible, but being the daughter of one of the most famous couples in the world had to come with some perks, like three nannies, a special daily schedule, and some pretty famous aunties.

MUM'S THE WORD

Maybe it was to protect little Blue Ivy, or maybe she just didn't feel she needed to do it anymore, but sometime around 2013, just as Beyoncé was becoming the biggest star of the moment, she **stopped giving face-to-face interviews**. She wanted her music and her art to speak for itself. She still appeared on the covers of dozens of magazines, released a documentary about herself called *Life Is But a Dream*, and was still making music, but the interviews stopped.

She didn't really need to worry about negative press, though, because by then Beyoncé had a whole swarm of people looking out for her: they call themselves the BeyHive (and call their idol Queen Bey). With a massive online presence, they are Beyoncé's most hardcore and devoted superfans. They've even developed their own vocabulary:

The Beyhive Dictionary

beyhydration: the gap between releases when fans are starved of new music from their Queen B.

digger bees: fans who scour the internet for news of Beyoncé.

honeybees: fans who like to praise their queen, and don't go on the attack.

wasps: anyone who dares to criticize Queen Bey.

killer bees: fans who attack the "wasps" by flooding their online accounts with bee emojis—they've caused some people to shut down their accounts completely.

stans: Beyoncé's superfans, i.e., members of the BeyHive.

The BeyHive is one of the reasons Beyoncé doesn't need to worry about press releases or social networking. Once Beyoncé releases something new to the BeyHive, they do the rest for her, sharing it with the world!

9   BEYONCÉ TAKES A GAMBLE

Back in the 1980s and 1990s, people bought their music in stores, in the form of vinyl records or shiny CDs that held a whole album of tracks. An album was like one long story, and each song was a chapter. Beyoncé would **never forget** the excitement of listening to the whole of Michael Jackson's *Thriller* album.

An album release was a big event; it was exciting. But the internet changed everything. Now that people could download or stream one song at a time, music sales were plummeting. **The album was dying.** At the same time, Beyoncé's superfans were begging her for more new music and she wanted to give them something really special.

I want to prove to myself and everyone else that you can have a baby and have a big career if you want to.

Starting work on her fifth solo album, in the summer of 2012, she took an unconventional approach.

Ready ... Steady ... Go ...

Beyoncé was such a star, she could work with practically anyone she wanted, so she rented a house for a month on Long Island in New York City and rallied some big-time music collaborators. A few months later, they were running late. Beyoncé and her team had wanted to release the album just after the US Super Bowl in February 2013 and just before the Mrs. Carter Show World Tour that was booked for April 2013, but that wasn't going to happen now.

It was coming right down to the wire and the album still wasn't finished, but Beyoncé had to start thinking about how to make its launch stupendously unique. Here's what she came up with in August 2013:

1. She would launch all the songs at once (unheard of—everyone thought releasing singles before the album was essential to drum up excitement).

2. She would avoid any songs being leaked before the release date (almost impossible—so many people were involved in the production).

3. She would create a visual album that had a video for every song (mind-bogglingly expensive and seriously time-consuming).

Then a near foolproof plan was hatched to keep the album under wraps and get the music directly to the fans—it was so secret that fewer than ten people knew about it. And it was as simple as this: no physical copies of the album would be printed before the launch. It would be released **online only**, on iTunes. Apple was one of the most tight-lipped companies in the world, after all. If anyone could keep this secret, they could!

The launch date arrived, and at 12 p.m. on December 13, 2013, the team at Parkwood were staring at their computer screens in New York, while Beyoncé was flying in to Chicago having just finished a show in Louisville, Kentucky. The big surprise was moments away.

Minutes later, Beyoncé's exhausted general manager hit refresh and finally saw what she'd been waiting for: the secret album (simply called *Beyoncé*) appeared on iTunes. Once she landed in Chicago, Beyoncé received the news with a huge sigh of relief. **She'd achieved the impossible.** As one of the most famous musicians in the world, she had released an entire album with no promotion, no leaks, and a ton of videos to keep the BeyHive happy for ages.

I wanted people to focus on the art and forget about the fanfare for a change.

And her gamble paid off. The album went on to break the record for the **fastest-selling album** on iTunes, becoming the best-selling album by a female artist in 2013.

A PIT STOP

But Beyoncé didn't have time to pat herself on the back. She was still in the middle of her Mrs. Carter Show World Tour, which wouldn't finish until March 2014. She did, however, manage to make a quick pit stop at one very large white house . . .

The Obamas (today they're the former President and First Lady of the United States) and the Carters had been friends for a few years. The Carters had rallied behind Barack's campaign for president in 2008 and raised millions for the 2012 campaign, and Beyoncé had sung at both presidential inaugurations.

Michelle and Beyoncé supported each other's charities, Barack described Beyoncé as a role model for his daughters, and they were even close enough to ask for favors . . .

So when Beyoncé was asked to perform at **Michelle's fiftieth birthday bash**—planned for January 18, 2014—it was a no-brainer. She hopped on over to Washington, slipped on her signature gold sequined mini-dress, waited for Barack to deliver his happy birthday speech to Michelle, then belted out some hits. After all that, she happily partied away with the guest of honor and a lot of other VIP guests.

Then it was back to business.

ON THE RUN

As if she hadn't racked up enough air miles already, once the Mrs. Carter Tour wrapped in March, Beyoncé and Jay-Z decided to hit the road together. Three months later, in June 2014, they set off on their joint On the Run Tour. They'd finally get to spend a couple of uninterrupted months as a family, with two-year-old Blue Ivy coming along for the ride!

Everyone wanted to see what kind of show the couple would put on, and ticket sales went through the roof, with whole stadiums selling out in minutes. As usual, Beyoncé made a splash with her costumes, opening with a fishnet and leather bodysuit from Versace that had taken a whopping **200 hours** to make! Jay-Z had some epic looks of his own, which he capped off with one of his signature gold chains. Pulling in about $5 million per show, the tour was a massive success.

With so much money rolling in, Beyoncé and Jay-Z could splurge on a few things . . . like mega-million-dollar mansions . . .

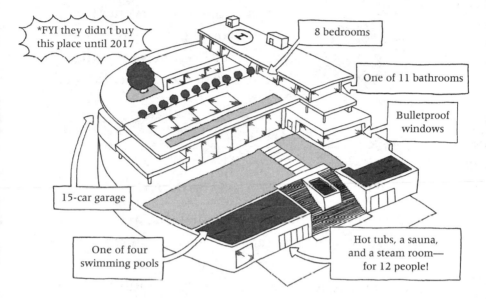

. . . a private island in the Caribbean (a twenty-ninth birthday present from Jay-Z to Beyoncé) . . . and fancy vacations in places like the Mediterranean.

By 2016, Beyoncé and Jay-Z were the highest-paid celebrity couple in the United States, raking in $107.5 million in that year alone. By all accounts, Beyoncé's got more money than anyone could ever need. Even her great-great-grandchildren are set for life!

Hey, I think I even said that in a song!

But Beyoncé never forgot that she'd had hard times growing up and that her parents had really had it tough! So it's no surprise that they gave some of the money they made from the On the Run Tour to charity. Giving back is something that Beyoncé has always done . . . She just doesn't shout about it.

Spreading Kindness

Since that first benefit gig for victims of 9/11, she'd been involved in plenty more worthwhile projects:

☆ Back in 2005, Beyoncé, Tina, Solange, and Kelly founded the Survivor Foundation to help the victims of Hurricane Katrina, a devastating storm that completely destroyed parts of Louisiana and Florida, killing around 1,200 people.

☆ In 2007, she helped set up food banks near the venues of her US tour, asking fans to bring food to give to communities in need.

☆ After playing troubled singer Etta James in *Cadillac Records* in 2009, she donated her entire $4 million salary from the movie to a drug treatment project. She and Tina set up a cosmetology center, training ex-addicts for a career in the beauty industry. She'd never forgotten the support and friendship she'd had in Headliners salon as a girl.

☆ And in 2013, during the Mrs. Carter Show World Tour, Beyoncé set up the #BeyGOOD charity initiative, which started out by supporting local causes in the cities where she toured. Now #BeyGOOD has reached as far as Burundi (helping bring clean water) and Nepal (fundraising for earthquake victims)!

A REALLY, REALLY BIG PLATFORM

It was the final few days before her big Super Bowl 50 halftime show performance in February 2016, and Beyoncé was chomping on some cheese puffs as she watched the playback of her rehearsal.

She'd been cajoled into the gig by her friends, legendary lead singer of Coldplay, Chris Martin (who was headlining), and pop sensation Bruno Mars.

She'd performed at the Super Bowl before, of course—back in 2004 singing the national anthem to start the game, and headlining the halftime show in 2013. She wasn't the headliner, but all eyes would likely still be on her . . .

Bruno Mars was sitting next to her. The two of

them would be performing together, and they'd bonded as they worked to get in shape for the big day, so he could not believe what he was seeing.

It's no wonder she was comfort eating; she was about to perform in front of tens of millions of people and shock the world (again) with **another surprise release**.

A new song, "Formation," from her upcoming album, would be released the day before the Super Bowl. "Formation" made a statement. It was about protesting against racism in the United States and celebrating Black lives. African Americans across US cities had been suffering from police brutality, and there was still a lot of racial injustice in the country.

Beyoncé wanted to show how strongly she felt about that, and she wasn't afraid to be a little daring in the process. She'd always spoken her mind in her music, though her songs were never really controversial. But she'd been working in the music industry for more than half her life, and **she had her own opinions**. She felt she should use her art to discuss social issues. She was about to step onto one of the most watched stages in the United States—it was as good a time as any to take a risk.

THE "FORMATION" PERFORMANCE: WHAT WAS IT ALL ABOUT?

☆ Beyoncé's troupe of backing dancers was dressed in black, with afros and berets—a reference to the Black Panthers, a civil rights group from the 1960s that had stood up against police brutality.

☆ When Bey and her troupe formed a large "X" shape on the football field, it could have been a reference to civil rights leader Malcolm X, who was assassinated in 1965.

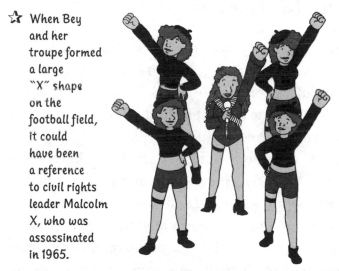

☆ Beyoncé's custom-designed leotard and warlike leather jacket (complete with a bandolier of bullets) looked remarkably like the one Michael Jackson had worn for his Super Bowl performance in 1993. A tribute to Michael? He was one of her musical heroes after all and one of the most popular musicians of all time, regardless of race.

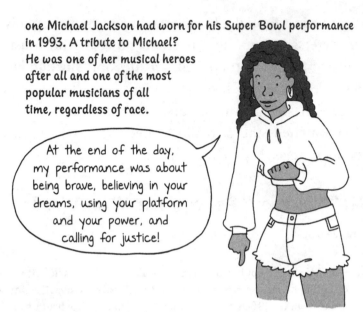

At the end of the day, my performance was about being brave, believing in your dreams, using your platform and your power, and calling for justice!

HOW TO MAKE LEMONADE

Beyoncé absolutely stole the show. The performance itself caused a sensation. Her fans thought it was a beautiful celebration of Black culture. Her critics thought it was **way too political**. Beyoncé certainly had a knack for keeping people talking.

Raised eyebrows finally started to lower, but on April 23, 2016, they shot up again, when she released the full album—*Lemonade*—and caused even more commotion. But before anyone could ask what the album was about, she headed off on the forty-date Formation Tour, leaving everyone to figure it out for themselves!

Lemonade was different from any previous Beyoncé album. It included:

☆ Twelve tracks accompanied by a stunning hour-long movie.

☆ Part of a speech by Malcolm X.

☆ Poetry by British-Somali poet Warsan Shire.

☆ Appearances from tennis star Serena Williams, young Black actresses, and mothers who had lost their sons to police violence, along with Jay-Z and Blue Ivy.

☆ A recipe for making lemonade.

It's about rocky relationships (something Beyoncé had never been eager to discuss in public), but it's also the story of Black women in America. The title was inspired by an amazing Black woman, Hattie White, who just happened to be **Jay-Z's grandma**! Describing her life, Hattie had said in a speech at her ninetieth birthday party: *"I was served lemons, but I made lemonade."*

A year later, at the fifty-ninth annual Grammys, Beyoncé was up for nine awards for *Lemonade*—including the biggest awards of the night: Album, Record, and Song of the Year! The only other artist nominated in all three categories was spectacular British singer-songwriter Adele, who had a total of five nominations.

Adele had been a **Beyoncé superfan** since the age of eleven, after she'd fallen in love with Destiny's Child's "No, No, No," and she didn't think an album could get much better than *Lemonade*. Along with everyone else, she fully expected Beyoncé would win Album of the Year, but here's what happened:

Adele walked off with the award in the end, but plenty of people agreed with what she'd said. Luckily, Beyoncé already had her name on a whole host of awards:

THE BIGGEST POP MUSIC AWARDS, EXPLAINED

American Music Awards: Created by American radio and TV legend Dick Clark, they are one of the annual "Big Three" music awards shows in the United States.

Beyoncé wins: 8, Destiny's Child wins: 5

Billboard Music Awards: Another of the Big Three, these are the awards of the people. To win one of these, or top the charts, you basically have to have the highest sales.

Beyoncé wins: 13, Destiny's Child wins: 11

Grammy Awards: The last of the Big Three, the Grammys are the gold standard in the music industry, awarded by the Recording Academy for musical achievement.

Beyoncé wins: 23, Destiny's Child wins: 3

MTV Video Music Awards: One of the coolest awards, these honor the best music videos.

Beyoncé wins: 4, Destiny's Child wins: 2

Soul Train Awards: These awards mean a lot for the African American community. They honor the very best of Black music and entertainment.

Beyoncé wins: 15, Destiny's Child wins: 4

TWINTASTIC

Beyoncé was a winner in other ways too. In 2017, she took the title for most-liked Instragram photo, with a whopping **11.18 million likes**! The post was nothing to do with her music; it was much more personal. She'd set Instagram ablaze by announcing she was pregnant with twins!

The Carter twins (a bouncing girl *and* a bouncing boy) were born on June 13, 2017. And she and Jay-Z kept up the family tradition of unusual names:

Now that Beyoncé was thirty-six and a mom of three, she took a little time off. She'd had some complications during her pregnancy and needed to heal, and she loved spending time with her new babies. She even renewed her marriage vows with her husband . . . and then eventually, she came back to the stage.

An Epic Year

Toot! Toot! All aboard! We didn't really expect Beyoncé to slow down, did we? She'd taken her break . . . and now 2018 saw her moving full steam ahead—with her family in tow!

☆ In April, she became the first Black woman to headline one of the world's largest and most famous music festivals, Coachella, in California. Her performance was so big (and historic) that they nicknamed that year's festival "Beychella." She even had a mini-reunion with Destiny's Child onstage.

☆ In June, Beyoncé and Jay-Z took off for the On the Run II Tour . . . before releasing their first joint studio album, *Everything Is Love.*

☆ In December, Beyoncé and Jay-Z hopped over to Johannesburg, South Africa, to headline a special show celebrating former president Nelson Mandela's 100th birthday. Sadly, Mandela had died five years earlier, but not before Beyoncé got the chance to meet him—at an AIDS benefit concert in Cape Town in 2004—an experience she said she would never forget.

Beyonce's Cape Town Outfit

bodysuit

Swarovski crystals

embroidered with a map of Africa's 54 countries

cape

SHE DID IT AGAIN . . .

Hardly slowing down as 2019 came around, Beyoncé **kept the world in the palm of her hand** by releasing a documentary film in April. She'd written, directed, and produced *Homecoming*, which was about her mind-blowing Coachella performance. The film includes quotes and inspiration from some of the most famous Black artists and intellectuals in recent history, and it came with an album, her third surprise album, also called *Homecoming*, which celebrates Black culture.

Michelle Obama was so inspired by it she sent Beyoncé a message via Twitter that said:

@MichelleObama

Keep telling the truth, because you can do it in a way that no one else can.

By now, Beyoncé had had a massive influence on music culture, but she'd influenced the world in some other surprising ways too:

☆ In 2016, students at the University of Texas could sign up for a class called "Black Women, Beyoncé, and Popular Culture."

☆ The name of a song she cowrote with Destiny's Child, "Booytlicious," is defined in the *Oxford English Dictionary*.

☆ Michelle Obama is such a good friend and fan that she dressed up as Beyoncé for the megastar's thirty-sixth birthday.

Beyoncé   Michelle

☆ Beyoncé even made her mark on natural history when, because of its beautiful golden abdomen, a species of Australian horse fly—*captia (Plinthina) beyonceae*—was named after her!

Beyoncé has never been afraid to push past her fears and dream big. When her big dreams are achieved, she dreams even bigger. It hasn't always been easy—she's had to work incredibly hard; she's made some mistakes and had some major disappointments along the way. But the **coolest thing** about Beyoncé is the powerful message she's sent to the world: chasing your dreams (even the wildest ones or the ones you've had since you were seven!) and taking risks can pay off big time. What incredible feat will she pull off next?

TIMELINE

Now that's what I call hard work!

1981
September 4,
Beyoncé is born in
Houston, Texas.

1988
Beyoncé first wows the
crowd at her school talent
show.

| 1980

| 1990

1989
Beyoncé becomes part
of a new girl band, Girls
Tyme.

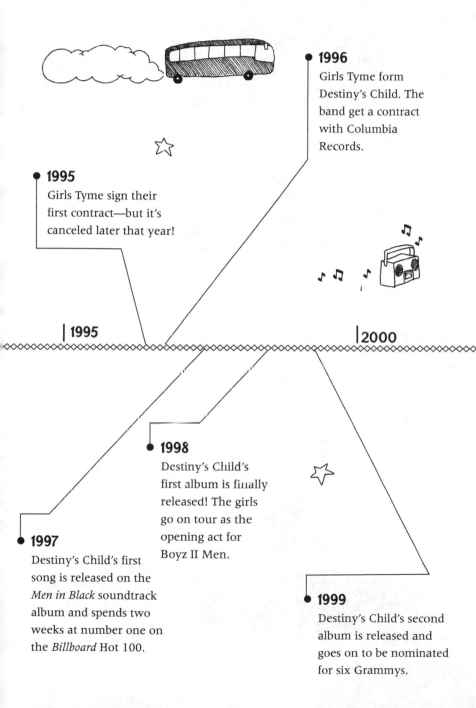

1996
Girls Tyme form Destiny's Child. The band get a contract with Columbia Records.

1995
Girls Tyme sign their first contract—but it's canceled later that year!

| 1995

|2000

1998
Destiny's Child's first album is finally released! The girls go on tour as the opening act for Boyz II Men.

1997
Destiny's Child's first song is released on the *Men in Black* soundtrack album and spends two weeks at number one on the *Billboard* Hot 100.

1999
Destiny's Child's second album is released and goes on to be nominated for six Grammys.

2000

Fans are shocked when Michelle Williams and Farrah Franklin join Destiny's Child, replacing LeToya Luckett and LaTavia Roberson. Farrah leaves just a few months later.

2001

Destiny's Child win their first Grammys and their album *Survivor* goes straight to number one.

Beyoncé films her first movie roles in *Carmen: The Hip Hopera* and *Goldmember*.

Destiny's Child start their world tour.

|2000

|2003

2002

Beyoncé is named Songwriter of the Year by ASCAP and starts work on her solo album.

2003

Beyoncé releases *Dangerously in Love*, which goes platinum and eventually sells over eleven million copies.

She begins her first solo tour.

2004

Beyoncé performs at the Super Bowl and the Grammy Awards show and wins five Grammys.

She announces her own clothing line, House of Deréon.

2007

The Beyoncé Experience, her third concert tour, happens this year.

|2006

|2009

2005

Destiny's Child perform their last show together on their final tour.

2008

Beyoncé marries Jay-Z in a super-secret ceremony.

"Single Ladies (Put a Ring On It)" is released and becomes Beyoncé's highest-selling hit.

Beyoncé sets up her own company, Parkwood Entertainment.

2006

Beyoncé finds her dream acting role in *Dreamgirls*.

2010
Beyoncé wins six
Grammys.

2012
Beyoncé and Jay-Z's
first child, Blue Ivy
Carter, is born.

| 2009

| 2012

2013
Beyoncé drops her secret
album: *Beyoncé*.

She performs at the
Super Bowl.

She launches the
#BeyGOOD charity.

2014
Beyoncé sings at Michelle
Obama's fiftieth birthday party.

2016

Beyoncé performs at the Super Bowl again.

Her groundbreaking album *Lemonade* is released.

She sets off on her Formation tour.

2017

Beyoncé and Jay-Z's twins, Sir and Rumi, are born.

2020

Time magazine names Beyoncé one of 100 women who defined the last century.

| 2015

| 2020

2018

Beyoncé becomes the first Black woman to headline Coachella Music Festival. She and Jay-Z start their On the Run II tour and release their first joint album, *Everything Is Love*.

Beyoncé and Jay-Z headline a show in South Africa, to mark what would have been Nelson Mandela's 100th birthday.

2019

Beyoncé's documentary film *Homecoming* and her third surprise album, also called *Homecoming*, are released.

She voices Nala in Disney's remake of *The Lion King*.

GLOSSARY

alter ego: A side of your personality that people don't usually see. Beyoncé's alter ego, Sasha Fierce, is like a character she plays onstage.

beauty pageant: A type of competition that started out with judges assessing contestants' looks but today usually includes tests of personality, intelligence, and talent.

Billboard Hot 100: A record chart that ranks songs based on sales, radio play, and online streaming across the United States.

blockbuster: A music album or film that is hugely popular and makes a vast amount of money.

Broadway: The group of theaters in New York City where plays and musicals are performed.

CEO: Chief Executive Officer: the most senior person in charge of managing an organization.

choreography: The art of making up dance moves and putting them in a routine.

compère: The host of an entertainment event.

composition: A song or piece of music.

discrimination: Treating people differently—and usually badly—because of, for example, their race, religion, gender, or sexuality.

empowerment : Giving people the power and control to do something—for example, vote.

endorsement: Approval or support, for example, if a company used Beyoncé's name to support its product.

harmonizing: The effect when different musical parts are being played or sung together.

headliner: The main performer at a show or concert.

inauguration: The act of someone officially taking on an important role, or the ceremony where this happens.

limelight: When someone gains the attention and interest of the general public, they are said to be "in the limelight."

The Mickey Mouse Club: An American TV show created by Walt Disney that featured a singing and dancing with Mickey Mouse cast of teen performers.

nomination: The act of putting someone forward, for example: to win an award or take on an important new position.

standing ovation: When an audience stand up and clap at the end of a performance to show their appreciation of it.

prejudice: An opinion formed, often before meeting someone, that isn't based on facts or experience but on an idea of what that person must be like.

retro: Similar to styles or fashions from the past.

scandal: An event that shocks the general public.

Notes

8   "A song . . . Let's hear it." Anna Pointer, *Beyoncé: Running the World—A Biography* (London: Coronet, 2014), 3.

10   "She can sing! . . . really *can* sing." Pointer, *Beyoncé*, 11.

68   "How y'all doing over here?" Jancee Dunn, "A Date with Destiny," *Rolling Stone*, May 21, 2001. See www.rollingstone.com/music/music-news/a-date-with-destiny-179775.

125   "I was served . . . made lemonade." Nick Levine, "Beyoncé Surprised the World with Her Most Powerful Album Yet," *i-D/Vice*, April 24, 2016. See i-d.vice.com/en_uk/article/8xn3xz/beyonc-surprises-the-world-with-her-most-powerful-album-yet.

126   "I can't possibly . . . so monumental." Luchina Fisher, "Critics Say Deck Was Stacked Against Beyoncé for Album of the Year," *ABC News*, February 13, 2017. See abcnews.go.com/Entertainment/critics-deck-stacked-beyonce-album-year/story?id=45460846.

131   "Keep telling . . . no one else can." Michelle Obama, Twitter post, April 18, 2019, 1:00 p.m. See twitter.com/MichelleObama/status/1118922383602192384.

Bibliography

Arenofsky, Janice. *Beyoncé Knowles: A Biography*. Rochester, NY: Greenwood, 2009.

Dunn, Jancee. "A Date with Destiny." *Rolling Stone*, May 21, 2001. See rollingstone.com/music/music-news/ a-date-with-destiny-179775.

Easlea, Daryl. *Crazy in Love: The Beyoncé Knowles Biography*. London: Omnibus, 2011.

Elberse, Anita, and Stacie Smith. "Beyoncé." Harvard Business School Case 515-036, August 2014 (revised October 2014).

Fisher, Luchina. "Critics Say Deck Was Stacked Against Beyoncé for Album of the Year." *ABC News*, February 13, 2017. See abcnews. go.com/Entertainment/critics-deck-stacked-beyonce-album-year/ story?id=45460846.

Hall, Michael. "It's a Family Affair." *Texas Monthly*, April 2004. See texasmonthly.com/articles/its-a-family-affair.

Knowles, Beyoncé, Kelly Rowland, and Michelle Williams. *Soul Survivors: The Official Autobiography of Destiny's Child*. New York: HarperEntertainment, 2002.

Levine, Nick. "Beyoncé Surprised the World With Her Most Powerful Album Yet." *i-D/Vice*, April 24, 2016. See i-d.vice.com/en_uk/ article/8xn3xz/beyonc-surprises-the-world-with-her-most-powerful-album-yet.

Pointer, Anna. *Beyoncé: Running the World—The Biography*. London: Coronet, 2014.

Simpson, Dave. "Beyoncé." *Guardian* (UK), November 4, 2003. See theguardian.com/music/2003/nov/04/popandrock3.

Taraborrelli, J. Randy. *Becoming Beyoncé: The Untold Story*. New York: Grand Central, 2016.

Webb, Robert. "Story of the Song: 'Crazy in Love,' Beyoncé (2003)." *Independent* (UK), November 14, 2008. See independent.co.uk/ arts-entertainment/music/features/story-of-the-song-crazy-in-love-beyonce-2003-1017557.html.

INDEX

Use these pages for a quick reference!

Be seeing y'all!

146

About the Author

Nansubuga Nagadya Isdahl was born to Ugandan parents in Cambridge, Massachusetts. After receiving a master's degree in diplomacy, she began working in international development in East and Southern Africa. She currently works as a technical writer and editor for international organizations as well as a children's book author. She lives in Tanzania with her husband and daughter.

About the Illustrator

Tammy Taylor is an illustrator who enjoys drawing children's books and comics. When she isn't drawing, she teaches others about comics and makes games. She lives and works in London.

"I dreamed up computer programming!"

Ben Jeapes ★ Illustrated by Nick Ward

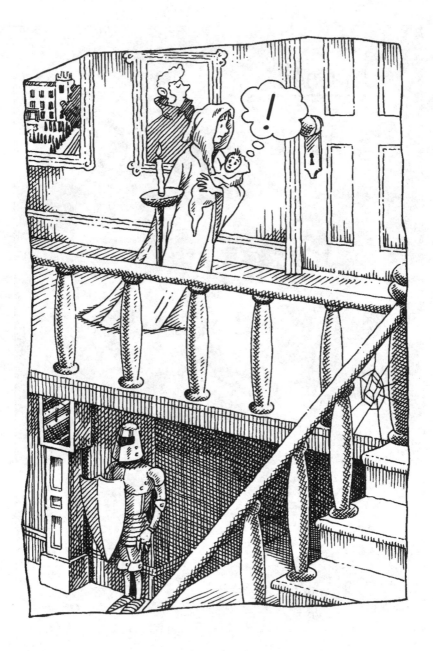

INTRODUCTION

13 Piccadilly Terrace, London, January 15, 1816

It was a freezing cold January night when **a one-month-old baby was being stolen** from her father. A woman took the baby from the nursery.

It was the wrong century for electricity and central heating. The bedrooms of the five-floor mansion were snug and warm with coal fires, but the stairs and hallways were as dark and cold as the night outside. The thief crept away with her precious bundle, terrified of being discovered. In a house this size, it was a long way from the nursery to the front door—a lot of wooden floors and stairs, ready to creak a warning.

The stairs bent under every step the woman took. She held her breath each time she put a foot down, feeling the wood flex under her weight. But no sound came.

Silver moonlight splashed across the tiles of the front hall. There was one more challenge—the big, heavy front door, bolted shut against the night. She drew the bolts back one by one and **the metallic clunks echoed around the house**.

One, *clunk*.

It was like an explosion in her ears. She made herself keep going. If people woke up, they would be pouring down the stairs any minute now.

Two, *clunk*.

The woman grasped the door handle and pulled.

Cre-e-e-a-a-a-k . . .

Heart pounding, she stepped out into the night.

The streets were cold, dark, and misty, but the city was already stirring, getting ready for the next day. It was very unusual for an upper-class lady to be out alone at this hour. **If she wasn't careful, she would attract attention.**

There was a carriage and a driver waiting for her. The woman hurried over and the driver helped her up. Once the door closed, she felt safer. He flicked the reins and the carriage lurched off.

The woman didn't relax until she reached her destination, a hundred miles away from London. But at least her plan worked. **She had successfully stolen her daughter** from her own home. The servants in the house would have obeyed her husband, the baby's father, and prevented her escape. A man's word was law, after all, and she knew they weren't completely safe.

In 1816, machines still ran on wind, steam, clockworks, or muscle power. Only a few scientists vaguely knew about electricity, and a "computer" was a person paid to do complicated sums—or computations—on paper.

This was the world the baby in the carriage was born into. Back then, machines were designed by men. Women in the nineteenth century had hardly any education and even less power. None of those male inventors would ever have imagined that, one day, one small machine might let you count and write, watch a movie, talk to friends, and more. But when the baby grew up, she wouldn't have been surprised at all.

One day, she would have a computer software language named after her, as well as a medal for people who have made great advances in the world of computers. **There's even a day named in her honor**, to celebrate women's achievements in science, technology, engineering, and math.

All in good time, though. At that moment, she was still only a month old!

Excuse me. Ada here. I'm the baby being stolen. The "thief" is my mother, Lady Annabella Byron, and she is not a common criminal!

Well, this was how your mother liked to tell the story . . .

Yes, but she believed she was saving me from my dreadful father, who gave an altogether different account of the event.

Hmm, your mom and dad were quite, erm, **interesting**, weren't they? Maybe we should start by talking about them . . . ?

Oh, my wretched family! Very well. Start a new chapter and tell everyone about them. But brace yourselves. It won't be pretty.

Read on in
ADA LOVELACE!